"This is a book that all of us need to read, especially in these days when everything around us seems to be unsteady and unsure. This is a book grounded in sustainable truth that will empower us to be more than conquerors."

Brady Boyd, pastor, New Life Church, Colorado Springs; author, *Addicted to Busy*

"This is without question Duane Vander Klok's best book so far. Writing accurately as he deals with real-life issues that people face, Duane makes no apology for addressing the devil, sin or personal responsibility. In a world where leading pastors are backing away from bold proclamations of the truth, this book is a breath of fresh air. I highly recommend this book to any believer who wants to grow in his knowledge of Christ and in his understanding of our authority over the devil."

Rick Renner, author, teacher; senior pastor, Moscow Good News Church

"After reading this book, I felt enlightened, encouraged and empowered. Not only does Duane Vander Klok do a masterful job at spelling out the extreme limitations God has put on the devil, but he also clearly reveals the incredible authority we have as believers. This is a must-read for anyone who is tired of being taken advantage of by the devil and is ready to live as an overcomer in Christ!"

Jimmy Evans, founder and CEO, MarriageToday

"Duane has been gifted with the ability to bring biblical truth to us in a relevant and practical way. He has done it here again! Enjoy!"

Dan Seaborn, president and founder, Winning At Home, Inc.

"*21 Things the Devil Cannot Do* gives powerful insight into who Satan is and your authority over him. It is packed with knowledge on how to resist the enemy and avoid giving him a stronghold in your life."

"Pastor Duane Vander Klok is clear and direct, exposing the deceptions that so many people have fallen prey to when it comes to who the devil is and what he can and cannot do. The devil is in the details . . . and the 'details' are under the feet of a Savior and Sovereign named Jesus and those who follow Him!"

"As believers, we need to be aware that there is a devil and how to handle him through our position in Christ Jesus. The enemy is trying to break up families. We need to be aware of who the enemy is so that he does not just knock the door down. *21 Things the Devil Cannot Do* is supernaturally practical, and we need this type of wisdom in order to defeat the devil."

21 THINGS THE
DEVIL
CANNOT DO

21 THINGS THE
DEVIL
CANNOT DO

DUANE VANDER KLOK

Chosen

a division of Baker Publishing Group
Minneapolis, Minnesota

Published by Chosen Books
11400 Hampshire Avenue South
Bloomington, Minnesota 55438
www.chosenbooks.com

Chosen Books is a division of
Baker Publishing Group, Grand Rapids, Michigan

Printed in the United States of America

Library of Congress Cataloging-in-Publication Data

Vander Klok, Duane.
    21 things the devil cannot do / Duane Vander Klok.
        pages cm
    Summary: "Pastor and TV host Duane Vander Klok exposes Satan's weaknesses and shows how you can use that knowledge effectively to defeat him in your life"— Provided by publisher.
    ISBN 978-0-8007-9616-7 (pbk. : alk. paper)
    1. Devil—Christianity. 2. Spiritual warfare. I. Title. II. Title: Twenty-one things the devil cannot do.
    BT982.V36 2014
    235′.4—dc23   2014031774

15   16   17   18   19   20   21   8   7   6   5   4   3   2

Contents

Foreword

Duane Vander Klok and I have been close friends and partners in ministry for many years. I realized as soon as I met him that Duane is passionate about God, his family and the family of God. So when he asked me to write the foreword for this book, I instantly said yes. As an author, I understand that a book's foreword serves two purposes. The first is obvious: I am recommending the book and explaining why someone should read it. The second purpose is not as obvious but is just as important: When I endorse a book, I endorse the author. Duane is a man whom I wholeheartedly endorse.

Some of my favorite books inspire me to fall more passionately in love with Christ and instruct me how to follow Him more closely. As I have traveled and become friends with many fellow authors, I have discovered that the books that connect me to God are written by people who are actively connected with and pursing Him. Duane is a man with a heart after God, and he has written a book that will help you follow Him.

I love the title, *21 Things the Devil Cannot Do*. As Duane details in the book, too many believers focus on and talk about what the devil can do. This only creates fear, but, as 2 Timothy 1:7 says, "God has not given us a spirit of fear, but of power and of love and of a sound mind." Please understand, I am not denying Satan's existence or claiming he is not a threat. Quite the opposite, as Scripture instructs us in 1 Peter 5:8 to "be vigilant; because your adversary the devil walks about like a roaring lion, seeking whom he may devour." What I am saying is that when we focus on how powerful and evil Satan is, we become too fearful because we have forgotten how powerful and good our God is.

When we do as Duane suggests, however, and focus on what the devil *cannot* do, we are really focusing on what God *can* do. More specifically, we are focusing on what Jesus accomplished on the cross and on what the Holy Spirit can do in our lives as a result.

On our own, we cannot achieve victory against the enemy; but when we receive salvation, we are forever victorious because Jesus is victorious. When He died on the cross and rose again, He defeated Satan. Revelation 12:11 says that the enemy is overcome by the blood of the Lamb and by the word of our testimony. Because Jesus shed His blood two thousand years ago, we now have a testimony about how He gave everything to save us. Because of what He did in the past, His Spirit presently lives in the heart of every Christian, ensuring a glorious future for His people and His kingdom.

How could the enemy possibly compete with that?

Robert Morris, founding senior pastor, Gateway Church;
bestselling author, *The Blessed Life*, *The Power of Your Words*,
The God I Never Knew and *The Blessed Church*

Acknowledgment

I would like to gratefully acknowledge writing consultant Trish Konieczny for her invaluable help in preparing this book for publication. Her skill, patience and sense of humor have made working together on this and other manuscripts a joy.

1

Sizing Up the Enemy

The Advantage Is on Our Side

Oh, it's only you."

So said the great evangelist Smith Wigglesworth one night when he awoke to see the devil standing at the foot of his bed. Far from reacting in fear and panic, as many a Christian might do, Wigglesworth sized up the enemy and found him lacking—so badly lacking, as Albert Hibbert writes in *Smith Wigglesworth: The Secret of His Power* (Harrison House, 1982, 1993), that the evangelist immediately rolled over and went back to sleep.

The devil must have been dumbfounded. No doubt he expected a different response, a little initial terror at the least. Had he foreseen such a scathing assessment, he probably would not have bothered to appear. Foresight, however, has never been one of his strengths. He cannot foresee anything, and he is not omni-anything either. Whereas God is omniscient, omnipotent and omnipresent—all-knowing, all-powerful and present everywhere—the devil is simply overrated.

Reports of Satan's power and ability are greatly exaggerated. The Body of Christ needs to follow Smith Wigglesworth's example in sizing up the enemy. We need to make an accurate assessment of who it is we face in spiritual warfare and what he can and cannot do. The list of things he *cannot* do is by far the longer list, and many of the things he *can* do require our permission first—which we need not give him under any circumstances. As the Word of God says, "Leave no [such] room or foothold for the devil [give no opportunity to him]" (Ephesians 4:27 AMP).

We are to give no place to the devil—no place in our lives, anyway. But there is one place we must assign to him: a place in our theology. If we do not give the devil a place in our theology, we can wind up in all kinds of trouble. Ignoring his existence is as dangerous as overrating him. People who completely ignore the devil often wind up blaming God for the disastrous things they experience. In reality, the source of their troubles is not God at all. Jesus made it clear in John 10:10 that the source of life's troubles is far different from the Source of life's joys: "The thief [devil] comes only in order to steal, kill and destroy; I have come so that they may have life, life in its fullest measure" (CJB).

John 10:10 is often referred to as the "great divide" verse: It divides God's loving character from the enemy's vengeful one, and it divides biblically solid theology from error. Put another way, it simply states, *Good God, bad devil.* That which blesses you and makes your life full and wonderful originates from God. That which steals from, kills or destroys a part of your life originates from the devil.

It is crucial to acknowledge that this malevolent being exists and that he is your personal adversary. This evil personality has rebelled against God and hates God. On his side are a host of helpers, known as demonic spirits, who rebelled with him. Since he and his host cannot harm God, they seek to harm those closest to God's heart: the humankind God created. That includes you and me. The devil's ultimate goal is our destruction spiritually, relationally, physically and in every other way.

Bad News/Good News

The bad news, then, is that we face a bitter personal enemy who hates us because we belong to our Creator. This enemy is wholly bent on our demise. Scripture refers to Satan as "the god of this world" (2 Corinthians 4:4 NLT)—note he is god with a small *g*! He and his demonic hordes have made it their first order of business to engender in this world a multitude of evils we all need to be delivered from. No wonder Jesus taught us to pray, "Deliver us from evil" (Luke 11:4 KJV).

The good news is that our Creator has not by any means left us to face this enemy alone. He sent us His Son, Jesus, as our Deliverer and King. Our King is not one to issue orders and stand back to see which way the battle goes—He came to fight the battle on our behalf. "For this purpose the Son of God was manifested, that He might destroy the works of the devil" (1 John 3:8).

Jesus accomplished what He came to do. His death, burial, resurrection and ascension secured victory over the enemy for us—which is the very reason the enemy hates the human race so intensely. Satan abhors the fact that Jesus came *in the flesh*, in human form like us, and defeated him. Was Jesus the Son of God? Absolutely. But in order to defeat the devil, He came—in a flesh-and-blood body—as the Son of Man.

Hebrews 2:14 (NLT) tells us why God chose to send His Son in human form:

> Because God's children are human beings—made of flesh and blood—the Son also became flesh and blood. For only as a human being could he die, and only by dying could he break the power of the devil, who had the power of death.

There is no doctrine in all the Bible that the devil hates more than that one—that a flesh-and-blood Man defeated the powers of darkness. Then, of all things, Jesus empowered His followers to do likewise in His name!

The devil and his demons therefore consider all flesh contemptible. It confounds and astounds them that God so deeply loves humankind that He would send His Son to us in human form to deliver us. In Scripture you do not read of many demons expressing their point of view, but in Job 4 one demon gives his assessment of humankind. He scoffs at those made of clay and says, "They are made of dust, crushed as easily as a moth. They are alive in the morning but dead by evening, gone forever without a trace" (verses 19–20 NLT). He says, in effect, "People are dirt! They're nothing but dust—so fragile that their lives can be extinguished the way an insect can be squashed. People are nothing!"

That is what the devil thinks about humanity. It galls him to be conquered by such a foe. It galls him so greatly, in fact, that he and his hordes will not even *admit* their defeat—they *will not* acknowledge that Jesus came in the flesh. They adamantly refuse. That stubbornness can be used as a test to identify them. Consider 1 John 4:1–3:

> Beloved, do not believe every spirit, but test the spirits, whether they are of God. . . . By this you know the Spirit of God: Every spirit that confesses that Jesus Christ has come in the flesh is of God, and every spirit that does not confess that Jesus Christ has come in the flesh is not of God.

I used this test myself while my wife, Jeanie, and I were missionaries in Mexico. For two of our years there, we lived with the Otomi Indians. From our Otomi village I would make trips into the mountains to preach. Often we would drive until the road disappeared, then get on mules and ride for hours to reach our destination, the little villages way back in the mountains. These villages were primitive—no electricity, no running water, no bathrooms—so we brought along our own supplies and equipment, such as a generator, a movie projector and big speakers.

After a twelve-hour mule ride to one such village, I headed to the church to hang wires for our equipment and get the church ready. Before long about a dozen of the village men showed up to hang around. Some of them watched and others helped me, but one particular man got on the platform and started speaking. I was busy hanging lights, and no one was paying much attention to the guy, but then I thought I heard him say, "One day Jesus just came to earth and appeared, *poof*, in a puff of smoke." I nearly dropped a lightbulb. I decided to listen more closely, and two or three minutes later, he said it again: "One day Jesus just appeared, *poof*, in a puff of smoke."

Saying that around me is like saying, "Sic 'em!" to a Doberman pinscher! I dropped what I was doing and climbed the platform. "I'd really like to pray with you," I said to the man.

"Oh, that's wonderful!" He beamed. "I have such great revelations when I pray."

I can imagine, I thought to myself, but out loud I asked, "Will you repeat a prayer after me?"

"*Sí!*" he said.

I started, "God, I love You."

"God, I love You," he repeated.

"And Your Son is wonderful," I went on.

"Oh, Jesus is wonderful," the man continued.

Then I said, "And Jesus came in the flesh."

"And Jesus came in the fl—, fl—, Jesus came in the fl—" he floundered.

This part of our prayer was not working for him. I noticed his eyes were starting to glass over and his voice was changing.

"Jesus came in the fl—, fl—, in the *spirit*!" he spat out.

The demon influencing the man *would not* confess that Jesus came in the flesh. That would have been confessing Satan's total defeat. I took the man out and commanded the demonic spirits to leave him in Jesus' name, and he was delivered.

Jesus came in the flesh and broke the power of the devil; then He gave us authority in His name to do the same. Above all, the devil fears that while we are still in the flesh, you and I will realize our God-given authority to break his power. This makes us dangerous to the demonic realm. The devil knows that when Jesus listed the signs that would follow those who believe, first on the list was "They will cast out demons in my name" (Mark 16:17 NLT). That is bad news for the kingdom of darkness.

Jesus wrought victory so that we would not need to live our lives in darkness, under the onslaught of the enemy. He bought us priceless blessings with His blood—salvation, healing, deliverance, peace and other blessings we will look at later. Because of Jesus' triumph, the enemy no longer has any claim to us. Our foe has been completely and utterly defeated, with no hope of a reversal.

For us, that is good news indeed! "[God] disarmed the principalities and powers that were ranged against us and made a bold display and public example of them, in triumphing over them in Him and in it [the cross]" (Colossians 2:15 AMP). It is finished, as Jesus Himself said on the cross . . . and yet, for all that, something still remains for us to do. We must *demonstrate Satan's defeat*.

Victory is ours—but only ours for the taking. We need to step in behind all Jesus has done and claim the results for ourselves. That is where our battle lies. "The kingdom of heaven suffers violence, and the violent take it by force" (Matthew 11:12). The war has already been won, but the army of hell is wholly unwilling to admit defeat. The victory must be *enforced*, and we must stand our ground, refusing to let the devil and his demonic hordes reoccupy territory that is no longer theirs.

God has given the Church authority in the name of His Son to do just that. Ephesians 3:10–11 says that "the manifold wisdom of God might be made known by the church to the principalities and powers in the heavenly places, according to the eternal purpose which He accomplished in Christ Jesus our Lord." In this verse, the Church is not a building but God's people. The "principalities and powers" refer to the enemy, Satan and his demons, just as they do in Ephesians 6:12: "We do not wrestle against flesh and blood, but against principalities, against powers, against the rulers of the darkness of this age, against spiritual hosts of wickedness in the heavenly places."

God's people are to make known to their enemy the wisdom of God and His eternal plans and purposes accomplished through Jesus Christ. God's plan is for the Church to demonstrate Satan's defeat—in short, for you and me to show the devil how it is going to be.

Hold the Fort or Storm the Gates?

Think about it: When you face opposition from the devil and his demonic hordes, do you demonstrate Satan's defeat? What do you demonstrate? Is it fight or flight? Which of these hymns rises first to your lips, "Hold the Fort" or "Onward, Christian Soldiers"?

Now, in a military battle there is great honor in holding the fort to the last man. Such an act speaks of the highest courage. In fact, Philip P. Bliss composed "Hold the Fort" in 1870 after hearing someone relate such an incident from the Civil War. But this is a spiritual battle we are talking about, and I would rather not find myself or my church in the position the hymn's next lines portray: "See the mighty host advancing,

Satan leading on; mighty ones around us falling, courage almost gone!"

It sounds as if we are cowering behind crumbling church walls, hoping against hope that Jesus will return and rescue us before the devil takes us all out. I much prefer the strategic position of the Church in "Onward, Christian Soldiers": "Onward, Christian soldiers! Marching as to war, with the cross of Jesus going on before. Christ, the royal Master, leads against the foe; forward into battle, see his banners go."

It is a question of who is leading the advance, who is following and who is giving way in retreat. In the first hymn, Satan leads his "mighty" host while the Church is barely hanging on, losing courage in the face of the enemy's ferocious attack. In the second hymn, Christ the royal Master leads the Church's soldiers into battle, and our foe is the one who must give way. The hymn continues: "At the sign of triumph Satan's host doth flee; on then, Christian soldiers, on to victory! Hell's foundations quiver at the shout of praise; brothers, lift your voices, loud your anthems raise. . . . Gates of hell can never gainst that Church prevail; we have Christ's own promise, and that cannot fail."

The scenario in the second hymn aligns with the Word of God. Jesus promised, "I will build My church, and the gates of Hades shall not prevail against it" (Matthew 16:18). As a soldier in this spiritual battle, you are not supposed to cower and yell, "Oh, God, the devil is after me!" Instead, your battle cry should be "Oh, God, I'm after the devil!" Your purpose here on earth is not to barely survive until Jesus comes back to rescue you. He has equipped His Church—you and me—to advance and storm the enemy's gates, plunder hell and populate heaven!

If that is not how you react in the heat of battle, the pages that follow will help you. You will see how to enlist in the advancing army of God and how to make the devil give way. You will learn to accurately size up the enemy and master weapons that have power to demonstrate Satan's defeat: "For although we do live in the world, we do not wage war in a worldly way; because the weapons we use to wage war are not worldly. On the contrary, they have God's power for demolishing strongholds" (2 Corinthians 10:3–4 CJB).

The Advantage Is All Ours

Our duty as the army of God is to demonstrate Satan's defeat. In any army accurate intelligence reports are vital for soldiers to effectively carry out their duty. In that regard, we have the distinct advantage. The source of our intelligence is the Word of God, which tells us everything we need to know to "fight the good fight of faith" (1 Timothy 6:12). With God's Word as our source, "Satan will not outsmart us," for we will be very "familiar with his evil schemes" (2 Corinthians 2:11 NLT).

We know that our adversary, the devil, "walks about like a roaring lion, seeking whom he may devour" (1 Peter 5:8). But we also know that we can put him to flight: "Therefore submit to God. Resist the devil and he will flee from you" (James 4:7).

In the Bible God personally speaks to each of us, and when it says the enemy will flee from you, it is not talking about him fleeing from some super-Christian. It's talking about *you.* You personally. You do not need to travel hundreds of miles to enlist the help of Billy Graham or Reinhard Bonnke. You do not even need to get your senior pastor out of bed. *You* have authority over the enemy in the name of Jesus.

The last time the enemy fled from you was the last time you resisted him. If that was a long time ago—or maybe never—here is the best part: The next time the enemy flees from you will be the next time you resist him. That can begin right now. *You* can begin to use the authority God has given you, the authority in Jesus' name, to demonstrate Satan's defeat in your life.

It is the devil's turn to be terrorized when Christians discover the authority they have in Jesus' name. The devil knows that once you learn to use that authority, your reaction to him changes from flight to fight—and his advance is routed. This book will help you learn to use your God-given authority over the enemy to experience that kind of victory. You will realize that the terror the devil inspires quickly fades in the light of the One whom you follow. God the Father gave His Son "the name above all other names, that at the name of Jesus every knee should bow, in heaven and on earth and under the earth, and every tongue confess that Jesus Christ is Lord, to the glory of God the Father" (Philippians 2:9–11 NLT). There is unfathomable power in that name!

You may be among those Christians who are absolutely petrified of the devil, hunkering down to barely hold the fort against him and his hordes. Or you may be among those Christians who know the war is already won but are still intimidated by the devil's tactics and unsure of how to deal with him. In either case, you need to know that the advantage is all on our side. You need an accurate, biblical perspective of the devil. Even more important, you need to know how to use the mighty weapons God has given us to demonstrate the devil's defeat.

Educating Ourselves about the Enemy

In the chapters ahead, we will educate ourselves about the enemy and discover who he is and who he is not. We will also discover a whole list of things the devil *cannot* do, and we will expose the tactics he employs against people who are unaware of his limits or ignorant of Scripture. Never was the verse "My people are destroyed for lack of knowledge" (Hosea 4:6) more accurate than in this area. People who lack knowledge of a biblical perspective on the devil allow him far more leeway in their lives than he has any right to take. When it comes to the devil, "Give him an inch, and he'll take a mile" is a gross understatement! But we need not allow him even one inch.

We will also examine a dozen signs of demonic activity and learn how to discern when "demon trouble" is afoot. Victory is at hand when we learn how to wield the mighty spiritual authority God has placed at our disposal and when we study the weapons of our warfare and learn how to become dangerous to the devil. We want to take every action possible to block the advance of his kingdom of darkness. Many of his tactics are only successful when people open the doors for him to unleash them.

Disarming the devil's attacks is frequently a matter of identifying the areas in people's lives in which they have ignorantly or inadvertently let him in. We will talk about how to pinpoint those areas and how to then *uninvite* the devil, ushering him out and firmly shutting the doors so he cannot come back. Jesus the Deliverer provided us with impenetrable spiritual weapons with which we can disarm the devil. Satan cannot get under, over or around them—he *must* give way to the mighty name of Jesus. Tactics such as knowing the truth, knowing in whose Kingdom we belong, resisting our enemy, putting on the righteousness of Christ and aligning our words with God's Word will make the enemy fall back in defeat.

Jesus completely defeated Satan and delivered us from every dark pit the devil would use to trap us. Along the way, our Deliverer demonstrated how we, too, can disarm the devil and live in God's light. That is a joy-filled victory worth shouting about:

> May you be filled with joy, always thanking the Father. He has
> enabled you to share in the inheritance that belongs to his people,
> who live in the light. For he has rescued us from the kingdom of

darkness and transferred us into the Kingdom of his dear Son, who purchased our freedom and forgave our sins.

Colossians 1:11–14 NLT

God has already rescued us and has enabled us to share an inheritance in the Kingdom of His Son. When we focus on Jesus as our Deliverer, understanding the blessings and tactical advantages He has already won for us, we can go on the offensive—we can demonstrate Satan's defeat.

2

Biography of a Defective Devil

The Enemy Has Fallen

"Know your enemy" is an ancient military principle based on the supposition that if you know who your enemy is and know his strengths and weaknesses, you are more likely to secure victory over him. That strategy has stood the test of time, and nowhere is it more applicable than in spiritual warfare. There is something you should know about your enemy, the devil—he is defective. His weaknesses far outnumber his strengths, and there are numerous things he simply cannot do.

Jesus the Deliverer has already defeated the devil at the cross of Calvary. This defeat has severely limited the ability of Satan and his kingdom of darkness to harm the crown of God's creation, humankind. Because its leader is already vanquished, the kingdom of darkness is fighting a losing battle. For every dozen things the devil does to trouble people, there are at least two dozen things he cannot do. We will look at 21 of those things in more detail shortly. Once you know your enemy, you will realize he is an unimpressive foe.

Is *This* the One?

According to Isaiah 14, one day we shall see the devil, and we "shall narrowly look upon" him (verse 16 KJV). In other words, we will squint—as if we cannot believe our eyes. We will all stare at him in amazement, asking,

> Can *this* be the one who shook the earth and made the kingdoms of the world tremble? Is *this* the one who destroyed the world and made it into a wasteland? Is *this* the king who demolished the world's greatest cities and had no mercy on his prisoners?
>
> Verses 16–17 NLT, italics added

The devil will be so unimpressive that we will be unable to fathom how he managed to hold whole cities and kingdoms in his grip.

According to God's Word, Jesus called the devil "a liar and the father of lies" (John 8:44 NLT). Satan would like people to believe he holds unlimited power and fearsome abilities, but that is a colossal lie. The devil is living a lie, and many people have believed it hook, line and sinker. He gets far more credit than he is due. When people see him, they will not be able to believe they fell for his charades.

The devil is not some all-powerful evil equivalent of God. That notion is dark-kingdom propaganda. God and Satan are not equal forces in opposition to each other—one good and one evil, one light and one dark, one Luke Skywalker and one Darth Vader. We have to expose such lies of the enemy to avoid falling for such propaganda.

Martin Luther did not fall for it. Yes, he knew the devil was real—when someone asked him, "Do you believe in a real, literal devil?" he is said to have uttered this insightful response: "Try resisting him awhile and *you* see if he's real." But Luther also knew the devil was no more than a fallen angel—a being created by God, but by no means the evil opposite of God Himself. In one encounter, when the devil showed up in Luther's study at Wartburg Castle, Luther did not get frightened—he got mad. In an outburst of anger, he hurled an inkwell at the devil, which smashed against the wall. The ink stain can still be seen today as a sign of how Luther drove the devil off in disgrace.

Who Is This Fallen Angel?

It is true that Satan *was* a powerful angel. It is also true that he can still wield a powerful influence, within certain limits. Let's look at a passage of Scripture that relates a little of the devil's history so we can better understand who he was at the time of his creation and who he has become since his fall. Ezekiel 28 contains a lamentation for the king of Tyre, who is a type of the devil, and it describes what the devil was like when God made him:

> You were the seal of perfection, full of wisdom and perfect in beauty. You were in Eden, the garden of God; every precious stone was your covering: the sardius, topaz, and diamond, beryl, onyx, and jasper, sapphire, turquoise, and emerald with gold. The workmanship of your timbrels and pipes was prepared for you on the day you were created.
>
> Ezekiel 28:12–13

Another name for the devil is Lucifer, which means "angel of light." According to Ezekiel 28, Lucifer certainly was an angel of light at his creation. He was magnificent to behold! He was covered with precious stones and adorned with "timbrels and pipes," which, according to Bible scholars, could refer to musical instruments. Some theologians suggest that his body actually contained musical instruments the way a pipe organ contains pipes. Others suggest that the day he was created, God fashioned special musical instruments for him. Whether or not Lucifer's body actually contained instruments, he was an especially gifted musician.

Some scholars suggest Lucifer's position in heaven was that of a worship leader or choir director of the angelic worship. Whatever the case, we know Satan was—and still is—musical. He understands and uses music. He knows music is potent, so even after his fall, he employs music as a means of influencing people.

As an aside, music can be a phenomenal tool for worshiping God, or it can be an insidious tool for inciting rebellion against God. Remember Daniel's friends Shadrach, Meshach and Abed-Nego and their ordeal in the fiery furnace? Their death sentence was a result of King Nebuchadnezzar setting up a golden image about ninety feet tall and commanding everyone that "at the time you hear the sound of the horn, flute, harp, lyre, and psaltery, in symphony with all kinds of music, you shall fall down and worship the gold image" (Daniel 3:5).

Nebuchadnezzar's subjects had the option of either worshiping his golden image or being thrown into the fiery furnace. But that unpleasant choice was not the sole factor motivating their idol worship: The music the king employed had its effect as well. Imagine the bellow of horns, flutes and stringed instruments filling the air in a symphony, and imagine the effect it might have had on Nebuchadnezzar's listeners. Because music powerfully affects them, people will do things in the presence of certain kinds of music that they would not otherwise do.

Music opens up something in a person's soul and spirit, making the choice of music you listen to vitally important. Some music can usher in negative effects, as did the music that led Nebuchadnezzar's subjects in their idol worship. Such music can be an important tool of the demonic realm. The music of godly, anointed people, on the other hand, can be a wonderful tool of the divine. It carries God's anointing: When David played his harp, for example, the terrible spirit depressing King Saul departed (see 1 Samuel 16:23).

Many times the Holy Spirit powerfully operates through music that draws people to worship God. In the midst of such music, the Holy Spirit can often reach someone who seems unreachable. Visitors to our church have given countless testimonies to that effect. The moment they heard the worship music, they were drawn by its reverence and the atmosphere it set. As a result of the music, many visitors felt a deep desire to draw closer to God even before they heard any preaching or a salvation call. Perhaps you have been similarly affected by music that glorifies God or seen the same effect in your own church.

Lucifer, the angel of light, was once familiar with such worship music. But then he changed his tune, as Ezekiel continues:

> I [the Lord] ordained and anointed you as the mighty angelic guardian. You had access to the holy mountain of God and walked among the stones of fire. You were blameless in all you did from the day you were created until the day evil was found in you. . . . So I banished you in disgrace from the mountain of God. I expelled you, O mighty guardian, from your place among the stones of fire. Your heart was filled with pride because of all your beauty. Your wisdom was corrupted by your love of splendor. So I threw you to the ground.
>
> Ezekiel 28:14–17 NLT

Humans are not the only ones with a free will. Angels are created beings, as we are, and they also have free will. They are not God's robots, as some people have been taught in Sunday school. If they were God's automatons, none would have rebelled. Angels can choose evil, just as we can, and some made that choice.

Satan took this opportunity, as did a third of heaven's angels, those who fell with him when he rebelled. Now they are fallen beings in rebellion against God. Since the devil and his fallen angels cannot succeed in their insurrection against God, they have determined to injure Him in other ways—by hating and hurting those whom God loves (again, you and me).

Lucifer is working with a vengeance to take down as much of God's creation as possible with him. Almost anywhere you go, a quick look around will confirm that he is at work and that he is often succeeding in his endeavors. But his success is temporary at best, for every time a child of God shows up to demonstrate Satan's defeat, his hollow victories are reversed. He is overcome by the blood of the Lamb and by the word of a believer's testimony (see Revelation 12:11), so he simply cannot do all the damage he desires.

Above all, the biggest thing the devil cannot do is win in the end. God has already declared Jesus the victor and decreed the lake of fire as the devil's end, as we will see when we look at Revelation 20:10 in the next chapter. "I am God, and there is no other; I am God, and there is none like me," God has declared. "I make known the end from the beginning, from ancient times, what is still to come. I say, 'My purpose will stand, and I will do all that I please'" (Isaiah 46:9–10 NIV).

Jesus told us, "Do not be afraid, little flock, for your Father has been pleased to give you the kingdom" (Luke 12:32 NIV). We have no reason to fear. The Kingdom is ours, and try though he might (and he will!), the devil cannot do anything to change that. I like that thought. In fact, I like thinking about all the things the devil cannot do!

Some of the devil's inabilities result from his fallen condition. They involve spiritual principles he cannot violate, and we will look at some of those in the next chapter, along with certain God-ordained laws that protect the Church and individual believers.

Some of the devil's inabilities are conditional and depend on the person or persons involved; for example, he cannot do certain things to a Christian who stands firm and resists him, although he wreaks havoc in someone else's life in those same areas when he is not resisted. In a couple of chapters we will examine a number of these conditional areas to learn how to stop him in his tracks when he tries to overstep his bounds.

The Lion outside the Walls

It may seem confusing that some of the devil's inabilities are conditional and some are not, but think of it this way: Our enemy is like a lion outside the walls; as we have seen from 1 Peter 5:8, he "walks about like a roaring lion, seeking whom he may devour." Yet God has instituted strong walls of protection around you and me and all His family of believers. Within those walls we are completely safe. Psalm 125 affirms it: "Just as the mountains surround Jerusalem, so the LORD surrounds his people, both now and forever. The wicked will not rule the land of the godly. . . ." (verse 2–3 NLT). If everything is as it should be, you stay inside God's protective walls and the lion—the devil—must stay outside. He can never overpower God or understand God's ways, so he can never prevail against the inviolate, unconditional spiritual principles of God.

Then there are those conditional weaknesses of the devil. In some areas, whether the devil can or cannot wreak havoc in your life is conditional on your behavior. You can cause breaches in the walls of God's protection around you by engaging in behaviors contrary to God's Word.

Unforgiveness, idolatry, the abuse of alcohol and drugs, illicit sex and other behaviors that violate God's laws break down your God-given protection from the enemy. Psalm 91:11 says when you are under God's protection, He will keep you in all

31

your ways, not all the devil's ways. You risk life and limb when you breach the walls of God's protection—there's a lion seeking an easy meal out there! We will talk more later about certain behaviors that you can choose or refuse, behaviors that open doors to the devil and give him opportunity to attack your life.

What about unbelievers? They already live outside God's protective walls, where they are constantly vulnerable to the lion's attack. Their lives are full of disaster and destruction because they have broken down the walls and walked into the wilderness. The devil devours them at will. God always stands ready, however, to extend His walls of protection around them—all they have to do is ask!

Each person is free to choose his or her own residence—whether inside God's protection from the enemy or outside it. The outside is a fearful place to live. A few chapters ahead, we will assess the damage the devil causes in people's lives who live outside God's protection. We will also strategize in chapter 8 about how to use the weapons Jesus provided to disarm the devil. But first, let's draw a line in the sand for the devil by clarifying 21 things he *cannot* do, particularly to believers inside God's protection. I think you will enjoy these next chapters as you discover how little power the devil actually has.

3

Spiritual Laws
the Devil Cannot Break

Some Things Never Change

In our constantly changing world, knowing that some things never change is a comfort. God Himself never changes, a truth of great comfort to His people. We can always rely on Him, always turn to Him, always expect that He will do all He has promised. "I am the LORD, I do not change," He assures us in Malachi 3:6. Hebrews 13:8 confirms it: "Jesus Christ is the same yesterday, today, and forever."

Because God does not change, the spiritual principles He has ordained are immutable—they stand the test of time and eternity. No one, neither the devil, nor his demons, nor God's angels, nor humankind, can circumvent what God has decreed. There are some spiritual laws the devil simply *cannot* break—also a truth of great comfort to God's people!

Let's take a closer look at some of these laws that have been ordained by God and are unbreakable for the devil. They make up the first nine in our list of things the devil cannot do. You and I can rest assured these things will never change.

1. The Devil Cannot Be Like God

"I will ascend into heaven, I will exalt my throne above the stars of God . . . I will ascend above the heights of the clouds, *I will be like the Most High*" (Isaiah 14:13–14, italics added). With these words Satan exulted in his heart as he rebelled against his Creator.

From the first moment of his rebellion, Satan has been a God wannabe. "I will, I will, I *will* ascend," Satan kept saying. It *will not* happen, however. God told him, in effect, "You *won't*!" The devil is not headed up—he is headed in the other direction. "You shall be brought down to Sheol, to the lowest depths of the Pit," God declared (Isaiah 14:15).

Almighty God has proclaimed, "Before Me there was no God formed, nor shall there be after Me. I, even I, am the LORD, and besides Me there is no savior" (Isaiah 43:10–11). There were no gods before the Lord, there will be none after Him. He is the only Savior, an unchanging spiritual principle the devil will not acknowledge—at least not at present. The devil longs for the worship and allegiance that belong to the Lord alone, yet he will never be worthy of them. He is nothing like God. "Who is like the LORD our God, who dwells on high?" Psalm 113:5 asks. The answer: no one!

The Lord is loving, merciful, unchanging, all-powerful, all-knowing, our provider. He is El Shaddai, the One who is more than enough. The Lord is good; the devil is bad. I cannot comprehend why anyone would choose to serve the devil rather than the Lord for even one minute. Satan does not treat well those who serve him best. His purpose is to destroy people, whether they are God's followers or his own. He snuffs out even his own followers' lives as quickly as he can.

A good example of this principle is found in the nation of Haiti, long ranked the poorest country in the Western Hemisphere. According to the CIA World Factbook, Haiti is one of the twenty poorest countries in the world. Life expectancy for its people is terrible, in the low sixties for both men and women. Adult literacy is not even 50 percent, unemployment is more than 40 percent and 80 percent of Haitians live in poverty. The situation is not good!

In fact, a pastor and missionary raised in Haiti, Doug Anderson, has affirmed that Haiti is the only country in the entire world that has dedicated its government to Satan. This dedication took place more than two hundred years ago, he reported, by freedom fighters rebelling against the French colonial government, in a ceremony involving voodoo priests, the sacrifice of a pig and the drinking of its blood. In the intervening years, many say that demonic spirits have been consulted about political decisions and that those decisions have shaped the country's history.

Prior to winning its independence in 1804, Haiti was called the "Pearl of the Antilles" because of its beauty. It was France's richest and most productive colony. Since its independence, though, Haiti has been wracked with poverty and has been in a continual state of political upheaval.

Understand that I believe fighting for freedom is a noble pursuit. The fault did not lie in Haitians' desire for independence. The fault lay in their methodology. America, too, was once a colony struggling for independence, but the leaders of the revolution dedicated their cause to God, not the devil. When they won liberty, they established "one nation under God" and looked to Him to guide their young nation. The United States faces some serious economic concerns, but Americans' situation continues to be far more hopeful than the Haitians'.

The devil is a God wannabe for two primary reasons. First, he wants the worship that rightfully belongs to God. Second, he wants to gain people's spiritual allegiance—not for the purpose of blessing them, as God would bless them, but for the purpose of destroying them.

Some people maintain they can worship in whatever way they choose because "all paths lead to God." That is dark-kingdom propaganda. "The things which the Gentiles sacrifice they sacrifice to demons and not to God," Paul states in 1 Corinthians 10:20. No matter how many different ways people try to reach God, the Bible clearly states that only *one* way leads to the Father: through Jesus.

Jesus said, "I am the way, the truth, and the life. No one comes to the Father except through Me" (John 14:6). Buddha and Muhammad cannot get people right with God. Voodoo rituals and idol worship are abominations, and behind every idol is a demon spirit. When people worship anyone or anything else but God Almighty, they give their allegiance to the devil. That means they cannot give their allegiance to God.

"I do not want you to have fellowship with demons," Paul warned the Corinthians. "You cannot drink the cup of the Lord and the cup of demons; you cannot partake of the Lord's table and of the table of demons" (1 Corinthians 10:20–21). When people give their allegiance to the devil, they put themselves in serious danger. He wants their allegiance so he can more readily invade and destroy their lives, as he did with the nation of Haiti.

People have a nebulous idea that trying out various paths to reach God will enrich their lives and broaden their spiritual acumen. I call this being so open-minded that your brains fall out. People may visit a fortune-teller or a séance, a channeler or a tarot card reader in hopes of connecting with the spiritual. Those means certainly do connect them with a spirit, but it is not the Holy Spirit! It is a spirit of an entirely different sort, which the Bible calls a "python spirit": It wraps itself around them to crush them.

Paul and Silas dealt with a python spirit in an incident recorded in Acts 16. A slave girl, who was following them about Philippi, continually cried out, "These men are the servants of the Most High God, who proclaim to us the way of salvation" (verse 17). Though some preachers might pay for that kind of advertising, Paul was greatly annoyed by it. Addressing the spirit of divination in the girl, he said, "I command you in the name of Jesus Christ to come out of her" (verse 18). She was freed that very hour.

The Greek word for that spirit of divination is a "python spirit." Any time someone consults a spirit other than God for information or direction, a python spirit is given full access. It grabs hold and wraps itself around that person to choke and destroy him or her.

If you choose to walk down one of the many "alternate paths" to God, you will bring back some bad company from your spiritual explorations! Your worship and allegiance belong to God alone—anything less will kill you, for the devil cannot bless you. He cannot be like God.

2. The Devil Cannot Understand the Ways and Word of God

Though the devil is crafty and intelligent, he cannot understand the ways and Word of God. The Bible must be understood spiritually. Understanding comes through revelation knowledge from the Spirit of God to your spirit, not through mental exertion. You do not understand the Bible by being mentally smart, even if your IQ is 220. According to 1 Corinthians 2:14, "The natural man does not receive the things of the Spirit of God, for they are foolishness to him; nor can he know them, because they are spiritually discerned."

All the prophecies about Jesus coming into the world, being crucified, being raised from the dead and triumphing over the devil have been right there in the Word of God all along. Even the details of Jesus' death—His side being pierced, His bones put out of joint—were clearly foretold in Scripture. But 1 Corinthians 2:8 says none of the princes of this world knew or understood, "for had they known it, they would not have crucified the Lord of glory" (KJV). Had the devil understood how utterly defeated he would be at the cross, he never would have motivated Judas to betray Jesus or incited the Jews to crucify Him.

The devil played a role in the redemption of humankind without even knowing it! Even though his defeat was clearly written in the prophecies of Scripture all along, he did not "get it"—and he does not get it yet. That is why we must make it clear to him that he is defeated. We must demonstrate his defeat.

Put another way, the devil is a "carnal" devil. He understands the flesh and the natural mind. If you battle him in those arenas, you will lose every time. This is why Paul rightly informs us, "The weapons of our warfare are not carnal" (2 Corinthians 10:4). Carnal weapons do no good against the devil.

He is, on the other hand, clueless regarding the ways of the Spirit. The last thing he wants is an eyeball-to-eyeball encounter with a Bible-believing, Spirit-filled Christian who fights the good fight of faith (see 1 Timothy 6:12). A good fight is a fight you *win*, and when you fight the devil with faith, you emerge victorious.

In chapter 8 we will learn exactly what kinds of weapons we have at our disposal to fight the good fight of faith, and we will learn how to use them. When believers employ those spiritual weapons and stand on the Word of God, it fries the devil's brain. He cannot understand it because he cannot understand the ways or Word of God.

3. The Devil Cannot Resist the Name of Jesus

Nothing in all of creation exists that does not have to bow to the name of Jesus. That includes the devil. Jesus is "far above all principality and power and might and dominion, and every name that is named" (Ephesians 1:21). His name carries authority in three worlds:

> Therefore God also has highly exalted Him and given Him the name which is above every name, that at the name of Jesus every knee should bow, of those in heaven, and of those on earth, and of those under the earth, and that every tongue should confess that Jesus Christ is Lord, to the glory of God the Father.
>
> Philippians 2:9–11

Every knee "in heaven" must bow at Jesus' name. The same is true of all those "on earth," which is the human realm. And all those "under the earth"—the demonic realm—must also bow. The devil and his demons *must* give way to the name of Jesus!

The great preacher Lester Sumrall used to tell a startling story that illustrated this reality. He was told the story while visiting a village on the Indonesian island of Java. Everyone in the village, from the mayor on down, was Christian, and the village was known as a place of refuge where people being persecuted could come to live in peace and security. Many years before Sumrall's visit, a Dutch missionary settled in the village. She began going from hut to hut to preach the name of Jesus. "Jesus saves, Jesus heals, Jesus delivers, Jesus is coming again," she kept telling the villagers. After listening to her preach for a few days, a short, skinny Javanese man pointed his bony finger in her face and said, "You need to leave this village!"

"Oh no, I can't leave," she replied. "I'm here to tell the people God loves them. Jesus died on the cross for them, and they can be saved, healed and delivered."

"*I* am the village witch doctor, and *I* was here first," he informed her threateningly. "If anyone gets healed or delivered in this village, *I* do it. *You* leave!"

"I won't," she asserted. "And I'm not into witchcraft; I serve the living God of heaven."

"I know nothing about that, but I heard you talking about miracles. Miracles are my job here, so you leave!" he insisted.

She steadfastly refused, so the witch doctor declared, "Then we'll have a contest. The loser will pack up and go."

The missionary agreed, determined to stand her ground. Then she went about her usual business, while the witch doctor went home to fast and pray to the devil. Three days later she heard a knock on the door of her hut. A group of men stood outside, ready to escort her to a platform they had built in the center of the village. As they made their way toward it, she saw the entire village gathered there and the witch doctor on the platform. She was put up there, too, and he said to her, "This is it."

"This is what?" she asked.

"The contest," he replied. "Do you want to go first? Do something that shows your power."

"No, *you* do something," she challenged.

That might have been a mistake. The witch doctor laid on the platform, stiffened and started levitating knee-high right in front of her. She had never seen anything like it in her life, and it scared her. She stood there next to the floating man and prayed, *Jesus, help me! I just came to preach, but now I don't know what to do! Help me!*

Inside she heard God answer, *Get him down.*

God, how can I get him down? she asked.

She heard, *Knock him down. Put your foot on him.*

She immediately put her foot on the man and pushed down, and he sank like a rock. Then God told her, *Tell that unclean spirit to come out.*

She said, "Come out of him in the name of Jesus!"

The witch doctor writhed and frothed under her foot. After a minute he sat up, looked around and asked in a daze, "Where am I?"

That witch doctor had just spent three entire days fasting, neither eating nor drinking, and praying to the devil for power. Yet when the demon came out of him, he did not even know where he was or what day it was.

The missionary made the most of her opportunity, explaining to him, "These people all came here to see who is the most powerful. Jesus is Lord! Now, are you ready to receive Jesus, who died for you and rose from the dead? He will save you and forgive your sins."

"Yes, I want to be saved!" the witch doctor exclaimed.

She led him in a salvation prayer, and then asked, "Do you want the Holy Spirit?" She explained about the Spirit of God, and when the man heard she had the Spirit's power inside, he wanted it, too. She laid hands on him, and he was filled with the Holy Spirit and began to speak in tongues right there on the platform.

From that day on, the village's atmosphere changed drastically for the better. A decade later, when Lester Sumrall visited, he found the whole village was saved. The village mayor who told him the story of the missionary was, of course, the former witch doctor himself.

Everyone everywhere will bow to Jesus' name. For humankind, the only question is, will we bow now, voluntarily, or will we bow later because we must? I say, do it now! Recognize Jesus as Lord now and receive all He has for you. One of the greatest gifts He gives you is authority in His name. We will examine the astonishing implications of that gift in chapter 8, as we study a dozen ways to disarm the devil. There is total victory for us in the name of Jesus, and the devil cannot resist that name.

4. The Devil Cannot Stop the Power of the Gospel

"For I am not ashamed of the gospel of Christ, for *it is* the power of God to salvation for everyone who believes" (Romans 1:16, italics added).

Few people comprehend that the Gospel itself *is* the power of God. Most people think that God's power falls from heaven at special times—you pray in the power, you sing in the power, the power moves in a service. Those times are special, but the Gospel itself is the power of God unto salvation. When you believe the message of the Gospel, its power is available to you—the exact same power that brought about the resurrection of Jesus Christ. That is why the Gospel is good news!

When you believe, the devil cannot stop you from receiving what is rightfully yours in your "salvation package." Forgiveness of sin and eternal life are in that package. Healing, deliverance, peace of mind, joy and everything else you need are also in it. The devil cannot stop you from receiving all that God has provided. The devil could not stop the resurrection, either. If he could have, he would have, because so much of the awesome power of God was released on that day.

Think of the death, burial and resurrection of Jesus as a God moment in history. Any person can revisit that spiritually defining moment any time they have a need. The power in that moment—the same exact power that raised Jesus from the dead—is available to you whether you are sitting in your living room or singing in the church pew. Sometimes people think if they could just get God's attention, if Jesus would come down and touch them, it would solve everything. But the power in the resurrection is the same for you now as if you were standing at the foot of the cross or standing at the tomb when the angel rolled the stone away and Jesus walked out. In the same way that the devil could not stop the resurrection then, he cannot stop the power inherent in that event from flowing to you now. Whenever you revisit the Gospel, the good news of what Jesus did in that moment, *it is* the power of God made available for you.

Although the devil cannot stop the power of the Gospel, it is worth noting that people can stop it. If people are ashamed of the Gospel or are ignorant of its power, they will not receive the power even though it has been provided for them. A few years ago I was discussing divine healing with another pastor in my city. He brought up the subject and asked me what I believed. I told him, "Healing is God's will. This is where it is in the Bible . . ." I quoted him some verses.

He looked at me like I had two heads. "At our church," he said, "we certainly don't believe in that kind of divine healing!"

"Don't worry, then," I replied. "You won't be seeing any."

That pastor would have been ashamed to put notice of a healing service in his church bulletin. Note that it did not take the devil to stop the healing power of the Gospel from reaching his church. The pastor and his congregation simply did not believe. Jesus said that the signs in Mark 16:17–18, among which is laying hands on the sick and seeing them recover, would follow those who believe, not those who do not believe.

For believers, however, the Gospel *is* the power of God. The devil cannot stop that power.

5. The Devil Cannot Escape Revelation 20:10

According to Revelation 20:10, "The devil, who deceived them, was cast into the lake of fire and brimstone where the beast and the false prophet are. And they will be tormented day and night forever and ever."

Do you believe what that verse says? Despite Revelation 20:10 and Revelation 20:15, "Anyone not found written in the Book of

Life was cast into the lake of fire," many people do not believe in an actual lake of fire where the devil and his followers will spend eternity.

I believe it. My motto is, The Bible says it; I believe it; that settles it. The Bible says a big fish swallowed Jonah, so I believe that, too. Had it been written the other way around, that Jonah swallowed the big fish, I would have believed that! If something is in the Bible, it is true.

Revelation 20:10 is true, and personally I like it that the devil will one day be out of the picture for good. He has been on the scene far too long already. Genesis chapters 1 and 2 describe the Garden of Eden as heaven on earth, but as soon as the devil arrived on the scene in Genesis 3:1, so did death, sickness, war, pestilence, grief and sorrow.

The devil stays around for over a thousand chapters in the Bible before Revelation 20:10 mentions him for the last time. After the devil disappears for good, two more chapters finish the Bible. What happens in those? You guessed it—heaven on earth again! "God will wipe away every tear from their eyes; there shall be no more death, nor sorrow, nor crying. There shall be no more pain, for the former things have passed away" (Revelation 21:4).

When the devil tries to remind you of your past, remind him of his future. You may have done what the devil said you did, but you are not who the devil says you are. As a believer, "anyone who belongs to Christ has become a new person" (2 Corinthians 5:17 NLT). The devil cannot escape Revelation 20:10—but if you are a believer, you already have.

6. The Devil Cannot Get Saved

Why can the devil not escape Revelation 20:10 by getting saved? First, God's Word is true and does not change, and it says he will be condemned. Second, the devil cannot get saved because he lives in a spiritual body. Hebrews 1:7 says that God makes His angels spirits. Because they do not live in a physical, flesh-and-blood body, there is no salvation for the fallen angels. Look at Hebrews 2:14–15 (NLT):

> Because God's children are human beings—made of flesh and blood—the Son also became flesh and blood. For only as a human being could he die, and only by dying could he break the power of the devil, who had the power of death. Only in this way could he set free all who have lived their lives as slaves to the fear of dying.

Jesus had to come in a flesh-and-blood body to die for you, break the power of death and save you. He means for you to be saved *now*, before you die. For you there is a way of escape—if you accept it. You can only receive what Jesus did for you and be saved while you are in a flesh-and-blood body.

Many people have the notion that after they die, they can stand before God and start negotiating. "God, I am so sorry. You were right, I was living wrong. From now on it's going to be Your way." But that will not work. When people die, it is too late because they are no longer living in a flesh-and-blood body. Hebrews 2:16 says, "For indeed He does not give aid to angels, but He does give aid to the seed of Abraham." Salvation needs to happen while people are still living in a flesh-and-blood body. Spirit beings without a physical body cannot receive salvation. The devil is such a being; he can therefore never get saved.

7. The Devil Cannot Predict the Future

The devil cannot predict the future because he does not know what is going to happen. He believes he can outmaneuver God and change the future, but if he believed Revelation 12:10 was inevitable, I believe he would quit right now:

> Then I heard a loud voice saying in heaven, "Now salvation, and strength, and the kingdom of our God, and the power of His Christ have come, for the accuser of our brethren, who accused them before our God day and night, has been cast down."

If the devil read and understood the book of Revelation, he would already know we win.

Although the devil is a spirit, he is a finite being in the sense of being confined within time. He did not exist forever in the past; he was created at a specific point in time. Nor has he traveled into the future—but God has. God is not confined by time. He has no beginning or ending point in time. He has seen the past, and He already knows the future. He knows every problem you and I will ever face, and He already has an answer waiting for us. He filled His Word with promises for us to grab hold of by faith, so we can have victory over every problem, circumstance or situation that comes.

We need not worry about tomorrow, but the devil is fixated on it. Have you noticed that the occult is completely obsessed with predicting the future through horoscopes, tarot cards, Ouija boards, clairvoyance, crystal balls, reading tea leaves, reading palms and even reading animal entrails? None of it works.

The devil is no good at predicting the future. Neither are his psychics. Have you ever looked through those newspaper tabloids in the grocery store checkout line? One day I picked one up while Jeanie was paying for our groceries, and I glanced at an article titled "The Devil Lives in New Jersey." Right. Some who live in New Jersey may try to act like the devil, but that can be true anywhere.

If you bought one of those tabloids in January and read its predictions for the coming year, you could keep that paper until the next January and see how inaccurate it was. The devil knows what he *wants* the future to hold, and he certainly wants his plan for you to transpire in your life. If you really want to know what will happen in the future, however, and if you want to know what awesome plans God has for your future, grab a Bible. It is 100 percent accurate—always has been, always will be.

Recently, Jeanie and I were reading excerpts from a book written in the 1870s by William Blackstone. It was called *Jesus Is Coming*, and it sold a million copies. Back then there were only about fifty million people in America, so that would be like selling six million copies of a book now. In the 1870s Blackstone maintained that the Jewish people would go back to Palestine, inhabit their own nation and take possession of the city of Jerusalem. When people read that book in the late 1800s and early 1900s, they thought, *This guy is crazy!* Right next to his prophecy, though, he listed something like 82 Scriptures to back it up. Now it has all come to pass.

The predictions in the Word of God are always 100 percent accurate. When God foretells an event, you can count on it happening. People read those 82 Scriptures about the reestablishment of the Jewish nation for years and years and thought, *Those verses must mean something else.* People believed what we call replacement theology: "Those Scriptures don't mean Israel. The Church is Israel now, so they mean the spiritual Church will be established there, not an actual nation."

Israel is Israel. What God said He would do for the nation of Israel, He did. Blackstone read it in Scripture and foretold it. He was right not because he was a prophet but because he read the Bible and took God at His Word.

"Call to Me, and I will answer you, and show you great and mighty things, which you do not know," God says in Jeremiah 33:3. God knows what the future will bring, but the devil does not have a clue. The devil cannot predict the future—neither yours nor his own.

8. The Devil Cannot Operate in an Atmosphere of Praise

"Through the praise of children and infants you have established a stronghold against your enemies, to silence the foe and the avenger," says Psalm 8:2 (NIV). Praising God brings confusion into the demonic realm and releases angelic ministry. Praise shuts down the devil.

The devil and his kind cannot operate in an atmosphere of praise. I understand this well because I cannot operate in some atmospheres, either. My wife, Jeanie, was getting ready for a conference once, and I was teasing her and getting underfoot. All she had to do was pull out her bottle of hair spray and I was gone! Jeanie's hair spray is what I call male repellant. Praise is like that—it is demon repellant. When you release praise to God, it silences the enemy and the avenger (see Psalm 8:2).

In 2 Chronicles 20, we read of three nations that came against King Jehoshaphat at one time. At the news of the approaching triple threat, the king called a solemn assembly of all Judah and Jerusalem and urged the nation to fast and pray. The Lord answered their cry through a prophet: "Do not be afraid nor dismayed because of this great multitude, for the battle is not yours, but God's" (verse 15). So Jehoshaphat went down to meet his enemies, and he "appointed those who should sing to the LORD, and who should praise the beauty of holiness, as they *went out before the army*" (verse 21, italics added).

The choir did not stay in the temple during the battle or stand off to the side to do their thing—they marched at the *forefront*, singing, "Praise the LORD," as they went *ahead* of the fighting men and their weapons. The story continues: "Now when they began to sing and to praise, the LORD set ambushes against the people of Ammon, Moab, and Mount Seir, who had come against Judah; and they were defeated" (verse 22). The enemies of God were routed by His people's praise!

The same thing can happen today. If we will establish an atmosphere of praise when we are under attack, the devil will be stopped in his tracks. The kingdom of darkness cannot operate in an atmosphere of praise.

9. The Devil Cannot Withstand the United Assault of the Church

Jesus is coming back for a victorious Church, a "glorious church, not having spot or wrinkle or any such thing" (Ephesians 5:27). As that glorious, victorious Church, we have some special assignments to fulfill before Jesus returns. One assignment is demonstrated in the subtitle of this book: demonstrating Satan's defeat. Another is to plunder hell and populate heaven. As part of the Church in my city, I want to make it hard for anyone to go to hell from Grand Rapids, Michigan.

Jesus intends for each believer to be part of that assault on the kingdom of darkness. He did not just save us out of something, the kingdom of this world; He saved us into something, the Church. If there were no purpose for our lives other than to populate heaven once we are saved, then they could simply hold us all under the water when we get baptized and send us on our way! But God has a plan—we are to be part of a Church that attacks the fortresses of the enemy, knocks down the gates and rescues the prisoners of war. We all need to be part of that plan. The devil cannot resist our united assault.

Some Christians do not see it this way. They want to be lone rangers for God. "I can be as good a Christian at home," they insist. "I can find God by communing with nature a whole lot easier than by being with all those people." They want to take on the enemy all by themselves as some sort of special forces unit operating on its own.

Such lone ranger Christians are assuming a dangerous role. I love the outdoors, too, and you can draw close to God there, but the only thing you will become if you keep having church all by yourself is a flake. God does not employ any lone rangers. Over thirty times the New Testament tells us we need each other. We need to love one another, forgive one another, encourage one another, build one another up. "Let us think of ways to motivate one another to acts of love and good works," admonishes Hebrews 10:24–25 (NLT). "And let us not neglect our meeting together, as some people do, but encourage one another, especially now that the day of his return is drawing near."

When we stand alone, we fall. When we stand together in unity, it is a whole different story. Jesus told us the kingdom of darkness cannot withstand a unified army of God: "I will build My church, and the gates of Hades shall not prevail against it" (Matthew 16:18). The devil cannot withstand the united assault of the Church.

Up Close and Personal

All the devil's "cannots" described in this chapter involve God's laws and spiritual principles He has ordained. They are inviolate—the devil cannot break them and never will. He can never be like God or understand the ways and Word of God. He cannot resist the mighty name of Jesus or stop the power of the Gospel. He cannot get saved and so escape his fate in Revelation 20:10. He cannot predict the future, or he would have given up the fight long ago. And he cannot operate in an atmosphere of praise or withstand the united assault of the Church.

Those last two get a little more personal. They involve not only God and the devil but also God's people and the devil. We establish an atmosphere of praise to defeat the enemy, and we make up the Church that storms Hades' gates.

In the next two chapters, we will look at the rest of the "cannots" in our list. They get even more up close and personal because they involve the devil and the individual. It is essential to scripturally understand these limitations on our enemy because they involve areas in which ignorance or a mistaken perception can cost people precious ground in their good fight of faith. Some of them can even cost people their lives.

While we as believers are protected by God's laws, sometimes what the devil can and cannot do in our lives depends on the things we do or do not do. These are the conditional "cannots" I mentioned earlier. To go back to our example of the lion outside the walls, in some of these next areas we must decide whether we are making ourselves vulnerable to the lion's attacks or not. Are we staying safely within the walls of God's protection, or are we risking our lives with our decisions and behaviors?

Spiritually, each of us must make a choice to either step into the circle of God's protection or to stay outside it. For everyone, that choice starts with salvation. After that, believers are protected in so many ways that it is no wonder the devil tries to prevent people from experiencing salvation. He knows that once they step out of his kingdom, his hands are tied. They are out of his reach under God's protection. He no longer has free reign to wreak havoc in their lives—unless they allow it.

People's decisions and behaviors in these next areas can literally prevent or permit the devil's access into their lives. As we look in detail at the ways the devil's hands are tied, you will see why they are so important to understand. Learning exactly what the devil cannot do in believers' lives—and learning how to keep him from overstepping any of those boundaries in *your* life—are vital steps to protecting your spiritual health and strength. Let's take a look at the things the devil cannot do to you when you stay under the protection of the King of kings.

4

Things the Devil Cannot Do to Believers

You Are Protected by Law

Once you belong to God, you are protected by law—God's law—from the enemy. There are numerous things the devil simply *cannot* do to those who believe. As Psalm 121 promises, God's ever-watchful eyes are on His children: "He will not let you stumble; the one who watches over you will not slumber. . . . The LORD himself watches over you!" (verses 3, 5 NLT). The promise of His care goes on: "The LORD *keeps you from all harm* and watches over your life. The LORD keeps watch over you as you come and go, both now and forever" (verses 7–8 NLT, italics added).

The Lord carefully shepherds His sheep. When they follow His voice, they are safe from all evil. That is the place you and I need to be—under His watchful eye, safe within His flock. The enemy may prowl around like a roaring lion outside the flock and seek whom he may devour, but he will not find us easy prey. He is no match for our protector, the Good Shepherd.

Some sheep, though, are bent on straying from the flock. Outside the circle of the Shepherd's protection lies danger. As we continue down our list of 21 things the devil cannot do, you will see why the ones we are about to discuss are more dependent on you than on him. You are solidly safeguarded under your Shepherd's care, but make no mistake—the devil can and will attack a sheep that strays outside the protection of the Good Shepherd.

Young King Josiah strayed from under God's protection, and his story contains a painful lesson for us all. Josiah became king at 8 years of age and reigned for 31 years. During his reign, the Book of the Law was found. Josiah had it read to all the people, then he made a covenant with the Lord to do all that they had learned. Of Josiah the Bible says, "Now before him there was no king like him, who turned to the LORD with all his heart, with all his soul, and with all his might, according to all the Law of Moses; nor after him did any arise like him" (2 Kings 23:25).

If any sheep was a prize, it was Josiah. Yet he chose to stray in one vital decision. Necho, the king of Egypt, passed through the Valley of Jezreel to make war against another country, and Josiah decided to fight him. King Necho sent a message to Josiah, "What have I to do with you, king of Judah? I have not come against you this day, but against the house with which I have war; for God commanded me to make haste. Refrain from meddling with God, who is with me, lest He destroy you" (2 Chronicles 35:21).

The king of Egypt told Josiah very plainly that he was under orders from God and that Josiah ought not interfere, but Josiah was spoiling for a fight. "Josiah would not turn his face from him, but disguised himself so that he might fight with him, and did not heed the words of Necho from the mouth of God"

(2 Chronicles 35:22). In the ensuing battle, an archer pierced Josiah with a fatal wound, and he died.

Was Josiah a godly king? He was unparalleled—the Bible says there was no king either before or after him who was like him. Did God love Josiah? Deeply, right through it all. Did Josiah step out of the circle of God's protection? Yes. He even went so far as to disguise himself to do it. Josiah wound up in a place he should not have been, doing things he should not have done. His disobedience cost him his life.

The devil will try to get you in the wrong place, doing the wrong thing, too. That always opens the way for him to come in and attack your life. Therefore it is vitally important—it is a matter of life and death—to get to know the Good Shepherd's voice and follow Him. Under His protection, you are safe. When you know Him and obey His voice, you can rest assured that the devil cannot do any of the following to you.

10. The Devil Cannot Touch Your Spirit

When you are saved, the Bible says, you are sealed with the Holy Spirit: "Having believed, you were sealed with the Holy Spirit of promise" (Ephesians 1:13).

What does it mean to be "sealed"? When I was a child, my mother made jam. She would pour it into glass jars, and then she would pour a layer of wax to seal the jars. That way nothing from the outside—particularly dangerous contaminants that could ruin the batch or make us sick—could get in. That illustration is not quite comparable to what the Holy Spirit does in you and me at salvation, but it gets the point across. The Holy Spirit plants the seed of God's nature in you at salvation, so that "no one born (begotten) of God [deliberately, knowingly, and habitually] practices sin, for God's nature abides in him" (1 John 3:9 AMP). The devil cannot contaminate God's nature in you.

I like how *The Message* describes what takes place in Ephesians 1:13: "It's in Christ that you, once you heard the truth and believed it (this Message of your salvation), found yourselves home free—signed, sealed, and delivered by the Holy Spirit." You are home free in Christ. Merriam-Webster's Dictionary defines *home free* as "out of jeopardy," and that is right where you are, no longer in jeopardy from the devil. The devil would have to go through the blood of the Lamb to get to you, but he cannot, so he cannot touch your spirit.

It is also harder for the devil to entice you to stray when you are sealed by the Holy Spirit. When you get saved, God puts His life, His love and His nature inside your spirit, and your spirit no longer agrees with sin. If you begin to stray into sin, you are miserable. The most miserable people on the face of the earth are Christians who live carnal, worldly lives. God's Spirit inside them is vexed by sin, and they know no peace. For good reason they have a relentless, nagging sense that danger is prowling around them.

I would much rather stay in the place 1 John 5:18 (NLT) describes: "We know that God's children do not make a practice of sinning, for God's Son holds them securely, and the evil one cannot touch them." When the Holy Spirit seals you at salvation and you stay under God's protection, the devil cannot touch your spirit.

11. The Devil Cannot Violate Your Free Will

Comedian Flip Wilson, playing his character Geraldine Jones in the early '70s, was famous for saying, "The devil made me do it." That catchphrase became widely popular, and sometimes you still hear people use it as an excuse for anything and everything. Really, though, the devil cannot *make* you do anything.

We often talk about the sovereignty of God, but there is also such a thing as the sovereignty of man. God gave each person a free will, and God will not violate it. Certainly He could do so, but He will not. For instance, if you want to stop and rob a gas station on your way home from work, God will let you. He does not want you to commit such a crime, but He will allow you to choose. He has given you the freedom to make choices—good or bad—about your life and behaviors.

God so esteems your free will that He will let you follow the devil and go to hell if you so choose. Again, He does not want you to be eternally lost; the Bible says God "desires all men to be saved and to come to the knowledge of the truth" (1 Timothy 2:4). But God will not violate the free will He gave you to choose your eternal home.

In the same way, God has absolutely prohibited the devil from violating your free will. So the devil came up with an alternate plan: He wants to weaken your will and hopefully get you to lay it down altogether. If he can attack your life and snare you into sin again and again, you come to the point that nothing inside you resists temptation. Your will becomes passive and you lay it down. Then the devil takes you captive. That is why 2 Timothy 2 says those who are in opposition to God need to know the truth, come to their senses and *"escape the snare of the devil*, having been taken captive by him to do his will" (verses 25–26, italics added). The only way the devil can violate your will like this is if you let him. You lay down your will by repeatedly sinning.

Two things happen every time you sin. The first is that your will becomes passive. The second is that your heart becomes darkened (see Romans 1:18–21). You can reach a place where you do not view sin as bad—in fact, you will view good as bad and bad as good, right as wrong and wrong as right.

It's not hard to find clear examples of this in modern society. If a person kills a spotted owl, for example, he or she may go to jail as a punishment. But if an abortionist, at the moment a baby is being born and the head is crowning, literally sucks the brains out of that infant in order to perform a partial-birth abortion, there is no punishment. According to darkened hearts, no crime has been committed. That is seriously skewed reasoning.

Remember when King David committed adultery with Bathsheba, impregnated her and had her husband murdered? In his prayer of repentance, recorded in Psalm 51, notice the two concerns he addressed in verse 10: "Create in me a clean heart, O God," he prayed. He knew his heart was affected—darkened— by sin, and he asked for a clean heart so that he could see sin for what it really was. Then he added, "And renew a steadfast spirit within me."

"Put spiritual strength inside me," David was asking, "so that when temptation comes I will say no." David knew he had to make a choice to say no to sin, just as we all do. He had to exercise his free will, not give it over to the control of the enemy.

The devil cannot take you captive to do his will—so long as you do not allow him to. The devil cannot violate your free will.

12. The Devil Cannot Possess What You Do Not Yield

Have you ever thought about why the devil goes around like a roaring lion, seeking whom he may devour? It is because he cannot devour just anyone. If he could, he would. But he must *seek*.

What is he seeking? In a word, access. He is looking for a way into someone's life, looking for what the Bible calls a "foothold." Access can come to him in many ways. He gains a foothold through fear, through sin, through unforgiveness, through ignorance, through the occult and in many other ways. Once his foot is in the door, he wreaks havoc in a person's life.

The devil can only access unprotected or yielded areas, though. God puts around every believer a barrier or wall that keeps the devil out. As we have seen, believers are protected by God-ordained spiritual laws. People can, however, weaken or break down their own wall of God's protection and give the devil a foothold. It is not smart, but people do it all the time.

You can give the devil a foothold in your sexuality by yielding to pornography. You can give the devil your tongue by yielding to gossip or lying. You can give him your mind by yielding to depression or negativity. You can give him your money by yielding to dishonest financial practices or by robbing God of tithes and offerings. You choose whether to yield certain areas or to post a "Keep Out!" sign for the devil.

"Whoever breaks through a wall will be bitten by a serpent," warns Ecclesiastes 10:8, a verse that talks about the risks of life. There is no greater risk to your life than breaking down your own wall of protection from the devil. If you give him access, he will come into your life. Rather than yielding ground to the enemy, obey God, live by His Word and resist the devil—and he will flee. The devil cannot possess what is not yielded to him.

13. The Devil Cannot Stay Where He Is Not Welcome

If the devil is not welcome in your life, he cannot stay. When you resist him and submit to God, he must flee.

If you make the devil welcome, though, he is within his rights to settle in for a long stay. The devil is almost like a stray dog (except his bite is worse than his bark). A friend whom I hunt with owns some acreage in the country, and he put a trailer on his property for an older woman who had nowhere to live. She settled in nicely. Before she knew it, a stray dog showed up at her door. She gave that dog a foothold (or maybe a pawhold) by letting it in and feeding it. Before she knew it, she had yielded her house to that dog! She had to move the furniture around to accommodate it, and she gave up her favorite spot because the dog claimed it. She spent money she had not budgeted to feed the dog, too, but she said it just would not leave. Was it any wonder? That dog was living in her warm house, eating her food and sitting in her favorite spot on the sofa. Why would it leave?

When you let the devil into your house (so to speak), feed him and make him warm and comfortable, he will not leave, either. You cannot participate with the devil by opening the door and then expect him to leave the nice, neat areas in your life alone. If you reserve a comfy spot for sin in your life in case you want to participate in it someday, the devil will come in and claim your whole house.

Nobody with good sense wants to feed a pet they cannot afford or house a pet that destroys everything in sight. Sin is that kind of pet. Sin lets the devil in, and he then bankrupts you in every way, destroying your life in the process.

You can submit to God and resist the devil; again, we will talk specifically about ways to resist him in chapter 8. They are effective because the devil cannot stay where he is not welcome.

14. The Devil Cannot Trespass Unless You Let Him

The devil cannot even trespass on your spiritual land, much less take up residence there, unless you let him. Once you reside in the Kingdom of God's Son, the devil has no legal right to set foot on your spiritual property.

The devil's domain contains sickness, disease, depression, grief, sorrow, bondage, sin and death of every kind, but you moved out of that miserable place at salvation. It is as if you put up a "For Sale" sign on your old life, and Jesus paid the asking price with His death on the cross so you could move to a better place.

The devil now has no right to impose his nasty stuff on you or dump his trash at your door. Look at my favorite translation of Colossians 1:13: "For he [God] has rescued us out of the darkness and gloom of Satan's kingdom and brought us into the Kingdom of his dear Son" (TLB). Clarence Jordan's version is another great interpretation: "For it was the Father who sprang us from the jailhouse of darkness and turned us loose into the new world of His beloved Son" (*The Cotton Patch Version of Paul's Epistles*, Association Press, 1968).

You and I were in a jailhouse of darkness and gloom before God rescued us and turned us loose into a new world. Imagine yourself standing on a beach, looking out at the vast ocean. Those little waves wetting your feet at the shore are what you have already experienced of the Kingdom of God—yet there is still a whole world of water out there. No matter how much of God you experience, there is always much more He has in store for you. As the Word says, "No eye has seen, no ear has heard, and no mind has imagined what God has prepared for those who love him" (1 Corinthians 2:9 NLT).

God's Kingdom is a world of freedom and forgiveness, healing and deliverance, righteousness, peace and joy. It is a world greater than your imagination can conceive. The world is at your feet, but Jesus said *you* hold the key to your new residence: "And I will give you the keys of the kingdom of heaven, and whatever you bind on earth will be bound in heaven, and whatever you loose on earth will be loosed in heaven" (Matthew 16:19). In other words, God will allow what you will allow in your life, and God will forbid what you forbid. Since He always respects your free will, it is up to *you* to put a "No Trespassing" sign on your new property.

Jesus called the devil a thief in John 10:10. Thieves break in where they do not belong and steal. What do you do if the devil or his forces try to set foot on your land or break in and steal from you? Point them to your "No Trespassing" sign and tell them where to go. Tell them, "Not in *my* life you don't; not in *my* body you don't; not at *my* house you don't; not with *my* finances you don't! I'm not sick; I'm healed. I'm not cursed; I'm blessed. I'm not below; I'm above—and by the way, devil, you are under my feet! I've moved out of the kingdom of darkness into the Kingdom of the Son of God. In Jesus' name, I command you to flee!"

As we mentioned earlier, one way you and I demonstrate Satan's defeat effectively is by keeping him out of the territory he has already lost. We need to defend our high ground in God. We cannot be weak-kneed, milquetoast Christians and possess the high ground—we have to take it and keep it by force.

Sometimes I think much of the Church wants to live on Easy Street. People want a responsibility-free religion where they can sit back and say, "*Que sera, sera*; whatever will be, will be. The Lord's will be done, and I'll let Him do it—I don't need to do a thing." In the gospels, though, we read that the disciples went out and, among other things, *drove out* many demons (see Mark 6:13 NIV). That tells me the demons did not want to leave, so the disciples had to *force* them out. Certainly not the Easy Street life!

We should not expect to live on Easy Street, either, at least not until we get to heaven, where the battles are over. In this earthly life attacks will come. Demonic trespassers will show up at our borders. The devil knows he does not belong on our ground—he just wants to see if *we* know it and if we will stand up for what we know. As Jesus said, "From the days of John the Baptist until the present time, the kingdom of heaven has endured violent assault, and violent men seize it by force [as a precious prize—a share in the heavenly kingdom is sought with most ardent zeal and intense exertion]" (Matthew 11:12 AMP).

Our victorious Christian life lived in the Kingdom of God is our promised land, and sometimes we have to defend it. The Israelites' Promised Land was a type, or foreshadowing, of our promised land. Think about this: God gave the Israelites their Promised Land, as He has given us ours, yet no one rolled out the red carpet for them when they arrived at the border. To move in and take possession of it, they had to face giants, conquer walled cities and then stand their ground against would-be invaders. The same will be true for you and me. We first have to take possession of our place in the Promised Land, which we do at salvation, and then we have to defend our rights in the heavenly Kingdom as a precious prize.

We are not living in the kingdom of darkness any longer, so the devil has no right to set foot on our land unless we let him. Each time we repel Satan's advances, we demonstrate his defeat and display one more thing he cannot do—he cannot trespass unless we let him.

15. The Devil Cannot Hide from the Word of God in You

The devil is the master of deceit. He tries to disguise himself, or even hide his existence, so he can take advantage of those who are ignorant of his devices. "My people are destroyed for lack of knowledge," God said in Hosea 4:6. Those who are ignorant of the devil perish first.

What you do not know about the devil can hurt you, which is why we are discussing at such length what he can and cannot do. What you know about the Word of God can save you, though. The devil cannot hide from the Word of God, and when you have the Word inside you, you are not easily taken in by Satan's schemes.

The ignorant are easily fooled by the devil. After all, he does not make a grand entry, lest he give himself away. He does not arrive at their door wearing a red suit, holding a pitchfork or sporting horns and a pointed tail. He does not say, "Go to hell! I'm here to show you the way."

The Bible says, "Satan disguises himself as an angel of light" (2 Corinthians 11:14 NLT). Sometimes he does that; sometimes he hides behind a smoke screen (no pun intended) as if he did not exist at all. He tries to deceive people into believing that the devil and the demonic have no effect whatsoever on their lives.

Even churchgoers are taken in by that deception. In the church I grew up in, we believed there was a devil because the Bible said so, but we thought he had nothing to do with our lives. We literally thought demons only existed deep in the jungle on a faraway continent. Missionaries might encounter them, but we were somehow protected by virtue of our location in a church in a civilized country. We were sure everything that happened to us, even trouble, was within God's plan for our lives.

If someone fell down the stairs, he would get up and say, "I'm glad that part of God's plan for me is over! I wonder what He's going to do to me next."

If someone got sick, she would say, "This illness is God's plan for my life. He wants me to suffer by carrying this cross of sickness, so I will."

We would pray for that sick person, "God, if it be Your will, heal her. (If not, take her.)" Naturally, we didn't say that last part out loud, but that is what it came down to all the same. We attributed everything, good or bad, to God. The devil was out of the picture completely—unless we were on a mission trip to the jungle.

If you think along those lines, too, then when you are sick, you have no business consulting a good surgeon about cutting the will of God out of you. If you have marriage problems and you think they are the cross God has for you to bear, you have no business spending time and money hiring a wise counselor to help you. If you think your kids are rebellious because it is a natural part of God's plan for teenagers, you have no business guiding them in a better direction.

If you think everything comes from God, you will not resist anything. When you carry that kind of thinking to its logical conclusion, the deception becomes obvious. The devil purposely promotes the lie that "everything that happens is God's will" so that he can escape people's notice and therefore preempt resistance on their part.

Not everything that happens comes from God or is His will. That is why Romans 12:2 urges, "And do not be conformed to this world, but be transformed by the renewing of your mind, that you may prove what is that good and acceptable and perfect will of God." When you renew your mind, you know the will of God. You are able to discern it, to look at a situation and say, "That's from God," or, "That's not from God—that's an attack from the devil and I must resist him."

You need to recognize when the hand of God is at work and when it is the hand of the enemy instead. You need to understand what things come from God and what do not, so that you will know what to accept and what to resist. That way, you can follow James 4:7: "Therefore submit to God. Resist the devil and he will flee from you."

"Do not be deceived, my beloved brethren," instructs James 1:16–17. "Every good gift and every perfect gift is from above, and comes down from the Father of lights, with whom there is no variation or shadow of turning." Whenever the Bible says, "Do not be deceived," it is because many people are prone to deception in the area under discussion. This passage in James is no exception. More people miss it here theologically than anywhere else. Good and perfect gifts are from God. He does not have blue Mondays. He does not have bad days when He gets mad and sends cancer. He does not break your leg just to show you He can! There is not even a shadow of turning in Him—what He sends your way is good and perfect. Destructive things come from Satan and are a result of the Fall.

When you know the Word of God and it has renewed your mind, you can make informed decisions about whatever

situations arise in your life. You will know the difference between God's path for you and the devil's sidetracking. The Word
of God inside you gives you discernment and helps you prove
the will of God. You will not be taken in by the devil's smoke
screen of invisibility, because he cannot hide from the Word of
God in you.

16. The Devil Cannot Get You to Blame God when You Know the Word

In the previous "cannot," we talked about how some people
attribute everything that happens in their lives to God while
leaving the devil completely out of the picture. Not only does
that deception make it impossible to know when to resist the
devil and for what, it also makes it easy to blame God.

The devil cannot get you to blame God for the bad things
in life if you know the Word of God. It is absolutely advanta-
geous to the devil to convince people that everything, both
wonderful and miserable, comes from God, because then he
can keep a lot of people *mad* at God. When people direct their
energies into feeling bitter against their Creator, on whom they
blame all their pain, they forget to resist the true source of their
hurt—the devil.

People who are busy being angry at God make no effort to
resist the devil. And if they do not resist him, he does not have
to flee from their lives. He continues to wreak havoc while they
blame the wrong source, their loving Creator, for their ills—a
very convenient state of affairs for Satan.

Consider Job, who had no Bible to read for discernment. The
account of his life in the book of Job is the oldest in the Bible.
Job could not consult any other part of the Bible, as no other
part had yet been written. When Job faced adversity, his mistaken
response was to blame his Creator. "He destroys the blameless

and the wicked," Job accused. "If the scourge slays suddenly, He laughs at the plight of the innocent. The earth is given into the hand of the wicked. He covers the faces of its judges. If it is not He, who else could it be?" (Job 9:22–24).

If God is not responsible for our pain, who else could it be? Like Job, many people's answer to that question is "God *must* be responsible for it!" We now know the correct answer to Job's question. Of course, we have the entire Bible to instruct us: It is not God but the devil who authors sickness, injustice and evils of every kind.

Not that Job was left clueless. God Himself enlightened him. "Who is this who darkens counsel by words without knowledge?" He demanded of Job (Job 38:2). Or, as *The Message* translation says, "Why do you confuse the issue? Why do you talk without knowing what you're talking about?"

In his misery, Job spouted off doctrine God called dark counsel. Much of the Church and the world still embrace Job's dark counsel today. We are living in what I call a theological mess in this regard. I have known so many people who want nothing to do with their God and Savior because they lay all the blame for their pain on Him. You probably know people like that, too. As soon as you mention God, they vehemently dismiss Him. "How could a loving God allow so much evil in the world?" is their general response. Then they get specific. "How could God allow my son to die from cancer?" "How could God allow my spouse to have an affair and walk out?" "How could God . . . ?" "How could God . . . ?"

Like Job, they do not understand that they are blaming the wrong source. Job 2:7 reveals the true source of trouble. Satan "struck Job with painful boils from the sole of his foot to the crown of his head." That is a crystal-clear indictment of the guilty party in Job's case, and that same guilty party is still causing the world's troubles today!

If the devil was not guilty of fomenting trouble, there would be no need to resist him. When he showed up in the Garden of Eden, so did sin, sickness, death, discord and every evil thing. When he disappears for good in Revelation, there is no more sickness, no more pain, no more tears. That says it all: *Good God, bad devil.*

Theology is as simple as that. Jesus demonstrated it Himself. Luke 13 relates an incident in which Jesus was teaching in a synagogue one Sabbath and caught sight of a woman who was bent over and could not straighten up. Scripture says she had been bound by a "spirit of infirmity" for eighteen years (verse 11). Jesus called her over and said, "Woman, you are loosed from your infirmity" (verse 12). She was immediately made straight and glorified God.

Note that this woman was not in a theological mess about the source of her trouble. First, despite her misshapen and perhaps painful condition, she was honoring God by attending the synagogue instead of blaming Him for her troubles. Next, she immediately glorified God when she was healed. She knew whom to thank for her deliverance.

The synagogue ruler was another story. Indignant that Jesus would heal on the Sabbath, he told the people to come get healed on some other day of the week—as if the healing itself were a bad thing rather than the disease. What interests us here is Jesus' response. "Ought not this woman, being a daughter of Abraham, whom Satan has bound—think of it—for eighteen years, be loosed from this bond on the Sabbath?" He demanded (verse 16).

This woman was not stricken with a sickness from God. Jesus' words make it clear Satan was the author of her sickness. Jesus did for her what He came to do for all who are oppressed of the devil—He healed her and set her free.

Your Bible says God wants you well. It says He wants you saved and healed and set free. When you know these scriptural truths from the Word of God, you also know who your real enemy is when trouble comes your way. You will not spend your life embittered at a loving God. When you suffer attacks of the enemy, you will not turn from your Creator in anger. Rather you will turn to God in hope. You will resist the devil and see him flee; then you will glorify God in your victory, as did the woman in Luke 13. The devil cannot get you to blame God when you know the Word of God.

Knowledge Is Power

We have covered some eye-opening ground in this chapter. God has set clear limits on our enemy, revealing to His children the many things the devil cannot do to a child of God. He cannot touch your spirit; he cannot violate your free will; he cannot possess what you do not yield; he cannot stay where he is not welcome; he cannot trespass unless you let him; he cannot hide from the Word of God in you; he cannot get you to blame God when you know the Word of God. Those are some powerful spiritual truths.

Knowledge is power, the saying goes. Knowing where we stand in relation to the devil gives us a tremendous advantage over him. This knowledge helps us take more ground for the Kingdom of heaven. It also helps us stand firm and keep the ground we take.

Knowing the devil's weaknesses fortifies us in our efforts to keep him in perspective and resist him. We will continue to expose the enemy's weaknesses in the next chapter. As we increase our knowledge of the defective devil, we will also increase our power to resist him and his deceptions.

5

Exposing the Enemy's Weaknesses

Our Victory Is Guaranteed

An exposé of an enemy's weaknesses is always a powerful thing. It replaces fear of the enemy with a confidence that he can be overcome. You may have heard the saying "Everyone has his Achilles heel." That is certainly true of the devil—except he has more than one Achilles heel. He has many.

Let's continue examining his many weaknesses by looking at the final "cannots" in our list of 21 things the devil cannot do.

17. The Devil Cannot Separate You from the Love of God

God loves you and me exactly the same as He loves Jesus. There is no difference. Jesus prayed in John 17: "I am praying not only for these disciples but also for all who will ever believe in me . . . so they may be one as we are one. I am in them and you are in me. May they experience such perfect unity that the world will know that you sent me and that *you love them as much as you love me*" (verses 20, 22–23 NLT, italics added).

God practices what He preaches. He told us to love our neighbors as ourselves (see Mark 12:31). Therefore, He loves us as much as He loves a part of Himself, His Son. When you love someone, you listen to them, notice things about them and think about their welfare. God listened to Jesus' prayers and knew everything about Him, and He does the same for you and me. Nothing we do escapes God's attention. He listens to us, He knows everything going on in our lives and He even numbers the hairs on our heads.

If you are not sure God loves you that much, your confidence in Him will wax and wane, leaving you on shaky spiritual footing. On Sunday you might dance around, enjoying a spiritual high, but by Tuesday you could feel down in the dumps. When you get a revelation of the love of God, though, it changes your whole perspective. It puts you on an even keel because *nothing* shakes your belief in God's love for you.

Paul knew we needed a revelation of God's love when he prayed for the church at Ephesus. Rather than praying the usual "Lord, bless them. Lord, protect them. Lord, do this or that for them," that we sometimes pray for each other, Paul prayed that the church would be filled with a revelation of the love of God:

Your roots will grow down into God's love and keep you strong. And may you have the power to understand, as all God's people should, how wide, how long, how high, and how deep his love is. May you experience the love of Christ, though it is too great to understand fully. Then you will be made complete with all the fullness of life and power that comes from God.

Ephesians 3:17–19 NLT

Paul understood God's marvelous love. That love encompasses you no matter what you have done, no matter where you have been.

The amazing thing about God's love is that not only is the devil unable to separate you from it, *you* cannot even separate yourself from it! This "cannot" is a little different from the others, then, because it is not dependent on what you do or do not do. Whether you are the greatest of saints or the worst of sinners, God's love for you remains the same.

You can never "step outside the circle" of God's love. Your sin cannot even remove His love from you—2 Corinthians 5:19 says in Christ God restored the world to Himself, no longer holding men's sins against them. Second Peter 3:9 says God is "not willing that any should perish but that all should come to repentance." That means Judas the betrayer could have gotten saved. Hitler could have gotten saved. No person has ever committed any sin that Jesus did not willingly pay for. God's love extends to anyone and everyone, even the highest VIP of sinners (a title Paul actually claimed for himself). People have only to receive God's love.

As Paul asked in Romans 8:35, "Who shall separate us from the love of Christ? Shall tribulation, or distress, or persecution, or famine, or nakedness, or peril, or sword?" Paul had to conclude,

> I am persuaded that neither death nor life, nor angels nor principalities nor powers, nor things present nor things to come, nor height nor depth, nor any other created thing, shall be able to separate us from the love of God which is in Christ Jesus our Lord.
>
> Romans 8:38–39

Nothing, least of all the devil, can separate you from the love of God.

18. The Devil Cannot Bless You

We have already learned why we are the devil's target. We are God's beloved creation, and nothing can separate us from God's love. Because the devil hates God but cannot hurt God, he is after us instead. In an effort to retaliate against God, the devil has purposed to inflict on us all the damage he can.

Thankfully, we are discovering in these chapters that the devil's power is extremely limited. The list of things he cannot do is long. An important point on that list is that the devil cannot bless you or me—never, never, never. You may sometimes be tempted to think serving God is hard, but beware—if you tried serving the devil for even one day, or a fraction of a day, you would soon find out what hard *really* is.

Proverbs 13:15 makes no mistake when it says, "The way of transgressors is hard" (KJV), and Romans 6:23 tells us the unequivocal truth when it says, "The wages of sin is death." Everything and everyone the devil touches tends toward destruction, bondage and decay. Decrease and not increase, curse and not blessing are always the result wherever he is involved. Nothing the devil touches ever tends toward good. The devil wraps himself around and squeezes the life out of everything and everyone he can—hence the name "python spirit" that we talked about in chapter 3.

A while back I was in Africa, and a missionary shared with our group an incident that had recently happened not far from his home. Some people walking down a road noticed a cab parked along the side. The door was open, but no one was inside. They took a look around the cab and found nothing, so they went a little way off the road to see if someone needed help. Not far from the road lay a python about twenty feet long. It took no notice of them, apparently preoccupied with digesting whatever made the huge, ominous bump in its middle.

When a snake that size eats a large meal, it cannot move for four or five days, so the people approached it and killed it while it lay digesting its prey. They cut it open and, sure enough, inside its belly was the cab driver who had been in the wrong place at the wrong time. The cabbie must have gotten out of his car and stepped off the road a short distance to relieve himself, and this python grabbed him. It wrapped itself around him, crushed him and ate him!

The devil wants you to meet the same horrendous fate. He wants to wrap himself around you, crush you and consume your life. To enable the devil to do that, however, you have to get into close proximity to him, like the cabbie who met the python in the bush just a few yards from his car. If you are traveling God's way, do not pull off the road and head into the bush where you do not belong. No matter what your reason, it is not good enough! To step off God's path for your life is to risk meeting up with the devil. Believe God's Word—the devil is out there seeking whom he may devour. No blessing awaits you when you step off God's path for your life.

Why anyone would risk an encounter with the devil by engaging in sin is beyond me. Sin makes you vulnerable to attack. It can put you in the wrong place at the wrong time far too easily. And sin always takes you further than you want to go, keeps you longer than you want to stay and costs you more than you can afford to pay, as the great preacher John Osteen once wisely said.

Even more, I cannot comprehend why anyone would actually choose to serve the devil for even one hour. He has no blessings to offer, and who would want any of his curses? Anything he promises is a lie. All he brings is failure, bondage and destruction. The devil cannot bless you.

The god of Islam, Allah, is a model for this principle. Some believe his name comes from the name of an ancient moon god, and that the crescent moon at the top of every Muslim mosque reflects this long history of Allah worship. Consider that no matter where Allah goes, he brings decrease and destruction, rather than increase and blessing. He is, in fact, a "desert" god, in that everywhere he shows up, it dries up. He is a withering spirit who reflects the source of all such spirits, the devil.

19. The Devil Cannot Keep You Depressed

This one is good news for everyone, Christians included. I am amazed at the sheer number of people who struggle with depression. The devil knows how debilitating depression can be, so it is a big gun in his arsenal of weapons. Depression is by no means an invincible weapon against you, even though it can seem like it when you are in the middle of it.

Depression is often (though not always) caused by a demonic spiritual attack on a believer's life. That is the kind of depression I refer to in this section—an occasional temptation to despair, an occasional bout with the blues. I realize that clinical depression of a more serious kind is a real and painful affliction for many, and I am not taking it lightly or condemning anyone in that condition. My goal is the reverse—to encourage and to help. I do believe, however, that clinical depression can also be spiritual in origin, or at least partly so. Some of the same principles that bring freedom in the mild bouts we are all prone to can also bring healing and freedom in more serious cases (though it is also wise to take a more careful look at the roots of clinical depression).

Whatever level of depression we are susceptible to, whether mild or severe, we need to remember the anointing on Jesus that Isaiah 61 mentions. One purpose for which Jesus was anointed was "to comfort all who mourn, to console those who mourn in Zion" (verses 2–3). Geographically, Zion is the mountain on which the city of Jerusalem is built, but in this passage it also refers to the Church. The passage continues, "To give them beauty for ashes, the oil of joy for mourning, the garment of praise for the spirit of heaviness; that they may be called trees of righteousness, the planting of the LORD, that He may be glorified" (verse 3).

I contend that God is *not* glorified when members of His Church look as if they have been baptized in pickle juice. *Heaviness* in this passage is an old English word that means "depression." Other meanings Merriam-Webster assigns to the word are equally grim: "dulled with weariness," "borne down by something oppressive," and "lacking sparkle or vivacity." When God's children display a spirit of heaviness, looking dull and weary with no sparkle in their eyes, they are no glorious reflection of Him. God is the Great Exchanger, though. To enable His children to be marvelous reflections of Him, He offers them a wonderful exchange: "the oil of joy for mourning, the garment of praise for the spirit of heaviness."

When Jesus went to the cross, God took our unrighteousness and gave it to Jesus, and He took Jesus' righteousness and gave it to us. He exchanged our sickness for His wholeness and our anxieties for His peace. God made many such exchanges with us at the cross, and each exchange was a good deal for us! So it is in the case of depression. We get the garment of praise in exchange for the spirit of heaviness.

Putting on the "garment of praise" not only glorifies God externally, it also does something inside of us. In Psalm 69:30, David revealed what happened when he praised the Lord: "I will praise the name of God with a song, and *will magnify Him* with thanksgiving" (italics added).

Thanksgiving magnifies God on our insides. Something happens internally when we rehearse our thankfulness to God out loud. We see God in a bigger way. He is always bigger than our imaginations, of course, but in the midst of depression or difficulty, our perception of Him tends to shrink. Thanksgiving clarifies our perceptions of God. It magnifies Him in our eyes.

Think of your thanksgiving as a magnifying glass you turn toward God. A magnifying glass does not literally make an object bigger than it already is, but it allows you to see the object better and more clearly. You cannot make God any bigger than He already is—the Bible says the universe cannot contain Him (see 2 Chronicles 6:18). Thankfulness, like a magnifying glass, enables you to see how much greater God is than any and every problem. When you are thankful, you begin to see God for who He really is.

As long as you see your problems as bigger than God, you are going to stay under those problems, borne down by something oppressive and dulled by weariness (as Merriam-Webster said). But whether your problem is as huge as clinical depression or as small as a bout of the blues, you can magnify the Lord in your heart through thanksgiving. That will cause you to see God as He truly is, *bigger* than your problem! You will break out of it with a sparkle in your eye and a vivacity, a zest for life in Christ as He sets you free.

I think that is why David provided us with a biblical protocol for coming into the awesome presence of God. In Psalm 100:4 he told us, "Enter into His gates with thanksgiving, and into His courts with praise. Be thankful to Him, and bless His name." David knew what would happen if we approached God with praise and thanksgiving in our hearts, with the right perspective. David knew God would be magnified in our sight.

Whenever we are under attack from a spirit of heaviness, we need to put on a garment of praise. When we begin to praise God, that spirit of heaviness cannot stay on us. Earlier we talked about how the devil cannot operate in an atmosphere of praise. Here is where knowledge really is power. We can turn that defect of the devil to our advantage when we are under attack. If we will take just five minutes to praise God and be thankful, and to do it out loud, the devil's campaign against us will be overthrown.

When you feel tempted to fall into depression, begin thanking God you are saved. Use your voice to thank God that you are forgiven and you are His child. Thank God that you are on your way to heaven, you are a joint heir with Christ and He is preparing a mansion for you in glory. Thank God you are healed, delivered, provided for and greatly loved with the same love God lavishes on His Son, Jesus. The devil and his hordes do not appreciate being reminded of who God is in your life and all He has done for you. They have no desire to listen to your praise session as you glorify your heavenly Father. They leave quickly and take depression with them. They are the ones who ought to be depressed anyway, considering the future they are facing.

You, however, have a glorious future awaiting you. As for the here and now, you receive the oil of joy in place of mourning when you put on the garment of praise. The devil cannot keep you depressed when you magnify the Lord with praise and thanksgiving.

20. The Devil Cannot Condemn You Unless You Let Him

"Accuser of the brethren" is the devil's name in Revelation 12:10. The name fits! He is always out to condemn people. He always brings up their past sins and failures. He reminds me of a grandparent eager to show off pictures of the grandchildren. Have you ever met one of those? If anyone talks to my wife about our grandkids, they had better step back and watch out for that heavy wallet of hers. She pulls it out and *flippp*, out fall dozens of pictures in those little plastic accordion sleeves: Gabe eating peas, Gabe drinking chocolate milk, Gabe fishing, twins Jazmin and Noah one day old, Jazmin and Noah two days old, Jazmin and Noah three days old . . . Jeanie has the pictures to show!

The devil is the same. He will flip out thirty pictures of you, thirty mental snapshots of different things you have done wrong. "This is your life," he gloats. "Take a look. You're worthless, good-for-nothing scum—not even a Christian, really. I have proof right here."

If you listen to the devil, he will condemn you. But you do not have to listen. He shows you your past to condemn you and make you feel hopeless, but you can just show him his future instead. Pull out a scriptural snapshot for him from Revelation 20:10, where he is thrown into the lake of fire forever and ever. That is not a pretty picture for him. Then tell him your future, the one Jesus described: "I go to prepare a place for you. And if I go and prepare a place for you, I will come again and receive you to Myself; that where I am, there you may be also" (John 14:2–3).

You have already been forgiven. "Having wiped out the handwriting of requirements that was against us," God has "taken it out of the way, having nailed it to the cross" (Colossians 2:14). Every sin you ever committed was nailed to the cross. There, God removed the "handwriting of requirements" that was against you and me.

Remember when Moses went up Mount Sinai and God wrote the Ten Commandments with the tip of His finger on tablets of stone? We refer to them as the Ten Commandments, but Jewish rabbis tell us there are actually 613 commandments in the Mosaic Law. They cover adultery, murder, lying, stealing, even what to do when you find your neighbor's donkey. Everything you can think of to do wrong is on that list.

God took that list, nailed it to the cross and said, "Here's why Jesus died; your sins are no more; you are white as snow" (my paraphrase). The Great Exchanger traded His Son's righteousness for our unrighteousness. Jesus was "delivered up because of our offenses, and was raised because of our justification" (Romans 4:25). We were justified in Him.

Think of the word *justified* as meaning "just-as-if-I'd" never sinned. "If we confess our sins, He is faithful and just to forgive us our sins and to cleanse us from all unrighteousness," 1 John 1:9 assures us. God promised long ago, "I will forgive their iniquity, and their sin I will remember no more" (Jeremiah 31:34). God has totally removed our sin and shame. "There is therefore now no condemnation to those who are in Christ Jesus, who do not walk according to the flesh, but according to the Spirit" (Romans 8:1).

The devil wants to nullify the exchange God made with you at the cross. He wants you to lay down your righteousness in Christ and pick up condemnation instead. Do not look at his wallet full of nasty pictures from your past. Decisively demonstrate Satan's defeat by keeping your eyes on the cross, the picture of how God defeated the devil. Hold on tightly to your righteousness in Christ. Satan cannot condemn you unless you let him.

21. The Devil Cannot Take You to Hell if You Do Not Want to Go

This final "cannot" of the devil is a special one—my favorite of them all. Because of all the things he cannot do—he cannot overpower your will, he cannot stop the power of the Gospel, he cannot possess what is not yielded, he cannot condemn you, and all the other "cannots" we have talked about—the devil simply cannot take you to hell if you do not want to go. If you do not want to have anything to do with the devil, you can be free of him for good.

How is that possible? In a word, Jesus. On your own you are certainly no match for the devil, but with Jesus as your King the devil had better watch out! When you choose to join the army of God, you are translated "into the kingdom of the Son of His love" (Colossians 1:13). And when you belong to

God, everything He has is yours, and everything you have is under His protection. To belong to God, follow Romans 10:9: "If you confess with your mouth the Lord Jesus and believe in your heart that God has raised Him from the dead, you will be saved." (If you do not belong to God but you would like to, turn to the salvation prayer at the end of chapter 9, which will help you take this step.)

In reality, getting saved means changing lords. Before you receive Jesus, you are under the domain of darkness. You are under the tyrannical rule of the devil and demonic powers—but they cannot keep you there if you want to be saved.

Everyone by default starts under the domain of darkness, but Jesus provided an escape. The fire-and-brimstone approach notwithstanding, the good news of the Gospel has never been a matter of scaring people into salvation by telling them, "You're a sinner going to hell! Repent or burn!" The good news of the Gospel is a matter of rescuing people by urging them, "You don't have to go to hell! It doesn't matter where you've been or what you've done. You have a way of escape, a way out of the darkness. You can be saved!"

You are free to choose your own lord. As Joshua said, "Choose for yourselves this day whom you will serve" (Joshua 24:15). When you choose Jesus as your Lord, you transfer your allegiance from the lord of darkness, the devil, to the Lord of light, Jesus Christ. A spiritual rebirth happens inside you, and you become part of a new Kingdom.

Jesus told a very religious man, Nicodemus, "You must be born again" (John 3:7). Nicodemus was as pious as they came, but he had not yet been born again. Despite all his theological head knowledge, despite his exalted position as a Pharisee, he had not yet chosen a new Lord for his life. Every single person needs to choose his or her lord. Being a "good moral person" is not enough and never will be. "For no one can ever be made right with God by doing what the law commands," Romans 3:20 reminds us. No one has ever gotten into heaven by being religious and obeying the Law.

It amazes me that entire churches are trying to do just that. They base their whole theology on being good moral people. You can ask multitudes in those churches, "Are you going to heaven?" and they will answer, "I *hope* so. I *think* so. I'm a good moral person, even better than most."

I asked one person if he was on his way to heaven, and he responded, "Well, I'm an American, aren't I?" *What does that have to do with it?* I wondered, but I suppose his was as good an answer as "I'm a Baptist, aren't I?" or "I'm a Catholic, aren't I?" or "I'm a Pentecostal, aren't I?"

Like Nicodemus with his Pharisaism, people hope the group they belong to will secure them a ticket into heaven. Membership in a particular denomination or in any group does not guarantee salvation, though. You must choose your Lord for yourself. You can attend your church every Sunday and still go to hell. You can be baptized in water sixteen times and go to hell. You can take communion and go to hell; you can sing in the choir and go to hell; you can be a good person and do all manner of good works and still go to hell.

The one thing you cannot do is receive Jesus as Lord and go to hell. The Bible promises, "If you confess with your mouth that Jesus is Lord and believe in your heart that God raised him from the dead, *you will be saved*" (Romans 10:9 NLT, italics added). The devil cannot stop you.

When you choose Jesus as your Lord, the devil loses all claim on you. You first "submit to God," and then you "resist the devil and he will flee from you" (James 4:7). He *must* flee because Jesus defeated him and "made a public spectacle" of him, triumphing over him at the cross (Colossians 2:15). And now, "He who is in you is greater than he who is in the world" (1 John 4:4).

Jesus' victory gave you full power and authority to demonstrate Satan's defeat in this most important of ways. If you are born again, you are living proof that the devil cannot take you to hell if you do not want to go.

Some Sinister Subjects

We have good reason to rejoice when we consider all the things Satan cannot do. We have covered a lot of ground with the 21 "cannots" in this book. In this chapter we discovered that he cannot separate you from the love of God, he cannot bless you, he cannot keep you depressed, he cannot condemn you unless you let him and—most wonderful of all—he cannot take you to hell if you do not want to go. As for me, knowing about the many things the devil cannot do is encouraging. He is not the all-powerful creature so many of us thought he was!

Shortly we will move into more sinister territory: things the devil can and does do to people who are unprotected, unwise about giving him footholds or living in ignorance about his schemes. We will examine the behavior of the Gadarene demoniac whom Jesus dealt with in the gospels, pinpointing a dozen signals in his life that indicated he was suffering from demon trouble. Those same signals of demonic activity are often present in people's lives today. Of course, Jesus freed the Gadarene demoniac, and we will also pinpoint a dozen ways we can follow Jesus' example and disarm the devil.

Before we move into that territory, though, I would like to cover another sinister subject. Many Christians are both wildly curious about and badly frightened by this subject, and there is a great deal of confusion about what the devil can or cannot do in regard to it.

For that reason, and because knowledge of the devil's traps gives you the power to avoid them, let's take a look at the topic of curses. There's no reason to be confused, because the Bible is clear about when a curse has power and when it does not. You might wonder, for example, if a Satanist can walk into your church and put a curse on it. (Has one ever tried? Such attempts have been made at our church, and I will tell you what happened.) How about someone putting a spell on someone else? Have you ever been afraid that someone involved in the occult put a hex on you? How do you safeguard yourself? A Christian does not need to be confused or frightened by these questions, as we will see in the next chapter.

6

The Question of Curses

No Cursing Allowed without Cause!

Some years ago during one of our church services, I was sitting on the platform during praise and worship and watching the crowd as we sang. A man four or five rows back caught my eye because he was moving his arms around strangely—up and down and all over the place. I thought, *This guy is a granola Christian*—as in fruits, nuts and flakes. Not a flattering term, I admit, but I had once talked to someone who was doing a similar thing with the arm waving, and she explained to me, "I'm weaving a glory cloud, Pastor." I thought that was a little flaky, so when I saw this new guy's wild gesticulations, I thought, *Oh great, here's another one.*

I got up to speak, and this guy kept doing his stuff even though he was now sitting down. On top of the arm gestures, he started speaking. He made so much noise that I had to keep talking as fast as I could to hold people's attention. If I paused for even a second, heads would turn toward the granola man. *I wish a deacon or an elder would haul that guy out or put tape over his mouth or something*, I thought. *He's badly disrupting this service.*

As the man kept up with his antics, I gave the quickest altar call in history. I urged people under conviction to raise their hands immediately, and I made them practically dash up the aisles in my attempt to keep things moving and keep the focus off granola man. I was worn out when the service ended. (Such disturbances in our church services are dealt with promptly now, believe me!)

After the service, some elders and ushers—politely—cornered the guy. Turned out he was a Satanist. He had attended our service in an attempt to put a curse on me and on our church.

You may be wondering what I did when I heard the sinister news. Did I pray and bind every kind of demon I could think of? Did I go on the alert for strange things happening around the building? Did I ask people to spend hours and hours in intercessory prayer? Did I fast for a week?

Nope. Nothing of the sort. I left the building and went home to eat a sandwich. Why was I not alarmed? Because I knew the Word of God promises in Proverbs 26:2 that "Like a flitting sparrow, like a flying swallow, so a curse without cause shall not alight." I had done nothing to open the door to the demonic or to give the devil a foothold. I had given no cause for a curse to "stick." I slept peacefully that same night, since I knew God also promises His children sweet sleep: "I will both lie down in peace, and sleep; for You alone, O LORD, make me dwell in safety" (Psalm 4:8). Demons and nightmares were the furthest things from my mind. I knew my church family, my family at home and I were all safe. I was not concerned about the incident, not one little bit.

A Curse without Cause Will Not Stick

Over my years as a missionary and a pastor, any number of people—Christian people—have approached me and said, "I think I've been cursed. Somebody put a hex on me. Help me!"

If you have ever thought that way, I want to tell you what I told them: A curse without cause will not stick. It cannot.

The devil and his hordes *cannot* attach a curse to God's people without cause. God's Word assures us, "No curse can touch Jacob; no magic has any power against Israel" (Numbers 23:23 NLT). What is true of the natural Israel is also true concerning the Church: "And now that you belong to Christ, you are the true children of Abraham. You are his heirs, and God's promise to Abraham belongs to you" (Galatians 3:29 NLT). The promises of Deuteronomy 28 belong to us. We will be blessed and not cursed, we will be above and not beneath, we will be the head and not the tail. As God's people, we are the blessed, the healed, the delivered, the anointed, the protected. We need to use our faith to believe what God's Word says about the question of curses. Hexes, spells and curses are all ineffective toward us.

There is not a devil, demon or Satanist in existence who can put a curse on God's children whom He has blessed. You need never concern yourself that someone will put an undeserved curse on you. It cannot happen. Your only concern need be that you might bring a curse upon yourself.

What do I mean by that? Did you notice that little phrase "without cause" in Proverbs 26:2? It says a curse "without cause" will not alight. But can you give a curse cause to stick? Can you somehow open the door to such an attack? Absolutely, or the phrase "without cause" would not be included in that verse.

How to Give a Curse a Cause

The book of Numbers in the Old Testament relates one story of how the Israelites, spiritually protected though they were, brought a curse upon themselves. At one point they had camped in the plains of Moab, and the Moabite king, Balak, saw their large numbers and was terrified. He did not want to suffer the same crushing defeat at their hands as the Amorites had, so he sent word to the prophet Balaam. "Look, a people has come from Egypt. See, they cover the face of the earth, and are settling next to me! Therefore please come at once, curse this people for me, for they are too mighty for me" (Numbers 22:5–6).

Balaam had a reputation for success. "I know that he whom you bless is blessed, and he whom you curse is cursed," King Balak flattered him (verse 6). That is not how it worked out for Balaam this time, though. He came to the king's aid, but this time he found himself powerless. To shorten a long story, the Lord opposed him.

Even Balaam's donkey opposed him. This is the one incident in all the Bible where it records that an animal spoke of its own accord. When Balaam was on his way to curse the children of Israel, his poor beast of burden kept seeing the angel of the Lord standing in their path with his drawn sword in his hand. The donkey tried every which way to avoid going ahead. It had enough sense to realize that you do not go where the Lord does not want you to go without serious consequences! It turned off the path and Balaam beat it; it pressed against a wall, which hurt Balaam's foot, and Balaam beat it; it lay down under its rider and refused to get up, and Balaam beat it. Finally the Lord opened its mouth, and it asked its master, "What have I done to you, that you have struck me these three times? . . . Am I not your donkey on which you have ridden, ever since I became yours, to this day? Was I ever disposed to do this to you?" (Numbers 22:28, 30).

Then the Lord opened Balaam's eyes, and he saw the angel, who immediately berated him for beating his donkey.

Why have you struck your donkey these three times? Behold, I have come out to stand against you, because your way is perverse before Me. The donkey saw Me and turned aside from Me these three times. If she had not turned aside from Me, surely I would also have killed you by now, and let her live.

Numbers 22:32–33

You would think knowing that the Lord, the angel of the Lord and even his own donkey opposed him would have given Balaam a clue that he was in over his head. He met up with King Balak anyway, though. Three times the king and Balaam came to a spot from which they could overlook the Israelites, and three times Balaam tried to curse the people of God. Three times he wound up blessing them instead. Balaam was forced to admit, "There is no sorcery against Jacob, nor any divination against Israel" (Numbers 23:23).

So far so good for the children of Israel, but the whole thing infuriated King Balak. The false prophet Balaam, however, had another trick up his sleeve. "*I* may not be able to curse the Israelites," he told the king, "but let me tell you how you can get them to bring a curse upon themselves" (my paraphrase). The Lord revealed Balaam's insidious plan to the church in Pergamos in Revelation 2:14: "I have a few things against you, because you have there those who hold the doctrine of Balaam, who taught Balak to put a stumbling block before the children of Israel, to eat things sacrificed to idols, and to commit sexual immorality."

Balaam advised King Balak to entice the Israelites to become involved in idol worship, then to entice them into sexual immorality. The Israelites fell prey to both evil strategies. Because they did not follow God's ways and refrain from such evil practices, they managed to bring a curse upon themselves, though the false prophet Balaam tried and failed to do so three different times.

Idol Worship Invites a Curse

This story of Balaam, Balak and the Israelites reveals two ways you can bring a curse upon yourself. The first is by involving yourself in idol worship of any kind. Any involvement in false religions opens a door to the occult, because behind all false gods are demon spirits.

New Age doctrines, Mormonism, the beliefs of Jehovah's Witnesses, Freemasonry and the order of the Shriners are all false religions. You might think some of those are "nice little civic groups," but beware—they have priests and altars and oaths. They are their own form of religion, whether their members admit it or not.

Perhaps the fastest way to bring a curse on yourself or open the door to the devil is by opening yourself up to some kind of false religion. Stay away from the occult and all its practices; stay away from Hinduism and the New Age movement; stay away from the meditation practices that come so neatly packaged in groups and classes here in the United States. Any dabbling in ideologies that lift up or worship something other than the one true God will lead you down a destructive road. The Israelites started by eating things sacrificed to idols, but they did not stop there. There is no such thing as a harmless exploration of alternate spiritual paths. They all wind up in the same place—the kingdom of darkness. And they all bring a curse, not a blessing, on your life. They give a curse a cause to "stick."

Sexual Immorality Invites a Curse

Balaam suggested a second way that King Balak might entice the Israelites to bring a curse upon themselves: involve them in immorality. Hence, the Moabites made friendly overtures to the children of Israel—*too* friendly—and look what happened:

> While the Israelites were camped at Acacia Grove, some of the men defiled themselves by having sexual relations with local Moabite women. These women invited them to attend sacrifices to their gods, so the Israelites feasted with them and worshiped the gods of Moab. In this way, Israel joined in the worship of Baal of Peor, causing the Lord's anger to blaze against his people.
>
> Numbers 25:1–3 NLT

Whenever people join themselves in the physical realm, a bridge forms between them in the spiritual, as well. In the next chapter we will cover this in more detail, but when two people unite physically, every spirit or bondage in one person's life now has access to both people. As a result, as soon as the Israelites joined themselves to the Moabites through illicit sex, the demonic spirit behind the Moabites' Baal worship made a connection to the Israelites' lives. Soon the Israelites were joining in pagan worship rituals, and the Lord's anger burned against His children as a result of their ungodly behaviors. They became cursed instead of blessed: a plague came upon them, and after all was said and done 24,000 had died.

Do not be seduced into bondage and a cursed life by illicit or perverse sexual practices. Any sexual involvement outside the God-ordained confines of a marriage covenant will inevitably lead to destruction. Rather than being "confining," sex reserved for marriage is actually liberating—it frees you from dangers such as the transference of spiritual bondages and from plagues such as STDs. Reserving sex for marriage frees you from a cursed life.

Anti-Semitism Invites a Curse

A third way to cause a curse to alight on your life is to participate in any form of anti-Semitism. When God promised to bring forth from Abraham a great nation, He also told him, "I will bless those who bless you, and I will curse him who curses you" (Genesis 12:3).

Abraham, his son Isaac and his grandson Jacob were the patriarchs of the Jewish people. If you hate the Jews, talk badly about the Jews or make trouble for them, God said He will curse you. That does not mean God will say four-letter words about you—it means He will shorten your life and remove His protection from you. You open the door to poverty, sickness and demonic oppression when you hate the nation of Israel.

Anti-Semitism is a demonic spirit. From the beginnings of the Jewish nation until now, this demonic spirit has relentlessly attacked God's people. We can see its activity in the way it possessed Haman, as recorded in the Old Testament book of Esther. You may remember how he tried to kill all the Jews in his country; instead, he was hanged on the very gallows he had built for the Jew Mordecai.

A little over seventy years ago, Germany's Adolf Hitler was possessed by this same spirit; as a result he tried to exterminate all the Jews in Europe. Hitler was responsible for countless atrocities, including the death of six million Jews, but in the end he was no more successful than Haman. Like Haman, Hitler's involvement with the demonic cost him his own life. His Third Reich, which he boasted would last a thousand years, only lasted twelve, after which he self-destructed by committing suicide on April 30, 1945.

God called Israel the "apple of His eye": "He who touches you [Israel] touches the apple of His eye" (Zechariah 2:8). The phrase *apple of the eye* poetically refers to the pupil or center, so in effect God was saying that anyone who attacked Israel was poking Him right in the eye. Not a wise thing to do! In another translation, God warns, "Anyone who harms you [Israel] harms my most precious possession. I will raise my fist to crush them" (Zechariah 2:8–9 NLT).

If you hate the Jewish people or the nation of Israel, you not only have a problem with God, you have a problem with the Savior. Think about it—Jesus has an ethnic heritage. He is Jewish. Mary, his mother, was a little Jewish girl. Joseph, his earthly father, was a Jewish carpenter. All twelve apostles were Jewish. Every single author in the Bible was Jewish. When you get to heaven, you will bow down and worship a Jewish

Redeemer. It is wise to honor those of His ethnic background now. God will bless you for it.

The Bible also says, "Pray for the peace of Jerusalem: they shall prosper that love thee" (Psalm 122:6 KJV). I believe one reason America has been so blessed in the past is because more than any other nation, America has stood with Israel. We need to pray that America takes a stronger stand with Israel, for all over the world a tremendously strong spirit of anti-Semitism is rearing its ugly head. I recently read in *USA Today* that many Jews are leaving Europe because of the persecution they face there, including beatings and murders and bombed synagogues. May that never happen here! We need to love and stand with the nation of Israel. If that is not where you stand politically, then you are standing against God and opening yourself up to a curse.

Robbing God Invites a Curse

A fourth way you can bring a curse on yourself is by robbing God. How can a person rob God? Malachi 3:8 spells it out: "Will a man rob God? Yet you have robbed Me! But you say, 'In what way have we robbed You?' In tithes and offerings."

If you neglect or refuse to honor God with your finances, you rob God. The next verse reveals the result: "You are cursed with a curse, for you have robbed Me."

Malachi 3 goes on to issue the only invitation God gives us to test Him. He says to bring all the tithes into the storehouse (that would be your local church), and as a result, "I will open the windows of heaven for you. I will pour out a blessing so great you won't have enough room to take it in! Try it! Put me to the test!" (verse 10 NLT). Beyond that inconceivable blessing, He adds, "And I will rebuke the devourer for your sakes, so that he will not destroy the fruit of your ground, nor shall the vine fail to bear fruit for you in the field" (verse 11).

For me personally, it is not that hard to choose between God's blessings and a financial curse. There is no contest. I shudder to think about living without God's protection on my finances, my livelihood and my family. All our Christian lives, Jeanie and I have followed God in this area, and He has proved Himself faithful. We live far better on 90 percent of our income with God's blessings on it than we could ever live on 100 percent under a curse! Yet many people do not believe this principle of the Kingdom, so they rob God and open themselves up to a curse.

Negative Words Invite a Curse

The fifth and final way I will mention that you can bring a curse on yourself is through the words of your mouth. Do you know how powerful the spoken word is? "God *said*, 'Let there be light'; and there was light" (Genesis 1:3, italics added). God *said*, and there was land; God *said*, and there were plants on the earth; God *said*, and there were lights in the heavens (see Genesis 1). God's spoken Word sets in motion amazing creative force.

Your spoken word sets creative force in motion, too. The Bible confirms it. "I create the fruit of the lips," God reveals in Isaiah 57:19. Proverbs 18:20 affirms it: "A man's stomach shall be satisfied from the fruit of his mouth; from the produce of his lips he shall be filled." The Amplified Bible puts it another way: "A man's [moral] self shall be filled with the fruit of his mouth; and with the consequence of his words he must be satisfied [whether good or evil]."

That can either be a scary thought or a wonderful thought, depending on what kinds of words you are in the habit of saying. The words you speak can bring forth either good or evil. You can go around saying, "Nothing ever goes right for me. My business attempts always fail. My family health history is terrible, so I will probably die young. My parents got divorced, so

I probably will, too." If that kind of talk is your pattern, guess what the pattern of your life will be? You will reap the harvest of your words and eat their bitter fruit.

On the other hand, you can go around saying, "God is blessing me! I have favor in my finances, favor at my job, healing in my health and strong family relationships. It doesn't matter anymore what my family history has been; I'm a new creation in a new family—I'm a child of God." Your life will bear out your words. It may take some time for you to turn old speech patterns around, and it may take some time for you to begin reaping a harvest from the good seed you sow with your words, but it *will* happen.

Positive, faith-filled words do something in the spiritual realm. For one thing, they please God, for "without faith it is impossible to please Him" (Hebrews 11:6). Faith-filled words move the heart of God. Negative words full of unbelief do something in the spiritual realm, too. Not only do they displease God, but they also give Satan license to try to bring those destructive things you are talking about into your life. Negative words bring on a curse.

Live a Blessed Life

As a believer, you need not be concerned about the devil bringing a curse on you while you are faithful in your walk with the Lord. The devil cannot bring a curse on the children of God. They are protected within the sheepfold, and their obedience gives a curse no cause to stick.

Live a blessed life by staying far away from the things that give a curse cause to stick. Flee any involvement in false religions, sexual immorality, anti-Semitism, robbing God or negative words. Any of these will open the door to the devil and can result in a cursed life. Flee sin of any kind. All sin brings a curse, for "the wages of sin is death" (Romans 6:23).

Obedience brings a blessing, and it also brings peace of mind. Walking in obedience, you will never need to say to your pastor, "Help! I think someone put a hex on me!" Even if you run into a devil worshiper on every corner and they curse you all day long, you can lie down and sleep peacefully at night, as I did after the Satanist incident at our church. You can rest assured that no curse will have an effect on you. It cannot.

Are you wondering at this point what it looks like when people *do* give a curse a cause? What happens when people open a door for the devil? After all our talk on the devil's weaknesses and the things he cannot do, it is time to consider the darker side of the demonic. Despite the devil's many defects, one look around us brings home the fact that Satan is obviously very busy these days on planet earth. You can clearly see that the people you know who live in ignorance of the devil's schemes are paying a heavy price for their ignorance. The devil and his hordes can and do influence, infiltrate and destroy the lives of people who live outside the protection we enjoy as believers.

How do you know when there is demonic activity in someone's life? What effects does it have on their behavior? Can the awful effects be reversed? Most important of all, what can be done to stop it? What does it take to disarm the devil? The chapters ahead will answer these important questions.

7

Uncovering the Enemy's Tactics

A Dozen Signs of "Demon Trouble"

D uring His time on earth, Jesus was in constant conflict with the devil. Literally from the day of Jesus' birth, the devil was trying to kill him. The devil was behind King Herod's horrible command to slay "all the male children who were in Bethlehem and in all its districts, from two years old and under" in an attempt to kill the King of kings (Matthew 2:16). After being baptized by John the Baptist, Jesus was led into the wilderness by the Holy Spirit. There the devil tempted Him for forty days, even trying to persuade Him to throw Himself down from the pinnacle of the Temple; Jesus fasted and withstood the temptation. When the devil could not catch Jesus in his traps, "he departed from Him until an opportune time" (Luke 4:13). After that, a significant part of Jesus' three-year ministry comprised the casting out of evil spirits. Even before going to the cross, Jesus was exposing the tactics of the enemy and demonstrating Satan's defeat at every turn.

Jesus' ministry consisted mainly of a few key actions—wherever Jesus went, He would preach and teach, He would heal the sick and He would set people free from demonic oppression. Matthew 8:16 gives one example of Jesus in action: "When evening had come, they brought to Him many who were demon-possessed. And He cast out the spirits with a word, and healed all who were sick."

The word *demon-possessed* in this verse is thus translated in most of our English Bibles; the term dates all the way back to 1611, when the new and uniform translation of the Bible ordered by King James I of England was published. Many leading Bible scholars and linguists of the day took part in translating the King James Version. At that time the English were tremendously fascinated with witchcraft and demons, and out of that cultural obsession came the translation "demon-possessed"; in reality, however, the Greek term could be better translated a number of different ways. Some Bible translations use "demonized," others say "under the power of demons" and still others say "possessed with devils." The word could also mean "to be vexed by a spirit" or "to be exercised by a spirit." Simply put, the Greek word used in Matthew 8:16 means "to have demon trouble."

People often think that someone with demon trouble will be a raving lunatic. While in some cases that might be true, demon trouble also covers a much broader range of issues and behaviors. People with demon trouble can range all the way from raving lunatics completely under the power of demonic spirits to average, normal people who are having trouble with their thought lives.

The amount of demon trouble in a person's life can vary greatly. The wise amount to put up with is none. Resisting the devil, however, requires an awareness of his schemes. He and his demonic forces are at the root of many issues in people's lives, but if people are unaware of how demon trouble can manifest itself, they are unable to resist it at its source. Once people can identify what demon trouble looks like, they are on their way to effectively putting a stop to it.

In the chapter that follows, we will take up the weapons that disarm the devil, but right now let's find out more about what demonic activity looks like. The story of the Gadarene demoniac in Mark 5 is one of Jesus' most famous encounters with demonic activity. The deeply troubled man in this story illustrated a dozen signs of demon trouble, and those same signs still show up in people's lives today.

The Man with the Unclean Spirit

The Bible does not reveal why the Gadarene man in Mark 5 developed demon trouble, but, as Proverbs 26:2 has shown us, "a curse without cause shall not alight." Demonic invasion always has a reason. As we saw in the previous chapter, it frequently stems from yielding to sin such as involvement in the occult or sexual immorality.

The latter probably occurred in the Gadarene's case, for Jesus called the spirit in him "an unclean spirit." That description is used 22 times in the New Testament. Each time it has to do with sexual perversion or illicit sex. The man was probably involved in some sort of illicit sex, and he wound up hosting a perverse sexual spirit.

Whatever the reason, demons began to invade the man's life. By the time Jesus visited the country of the Gadarenes, the man was in a terrible state:

> And when He [Jesus] had come out of the boat, immediately there met Him out of the tombs a man with an unclean spirit, who had his dwelling among the tombs; and no one could bind him, not even with chains, because he had often been bound with shackles and chains. And the chains had been pulled apart

by him, and the shackles broken in pieces; neither could anyone tame him. And always, night and day, he was in the mountains and in the tombs, crying out and cutting himself with stones.

Mark 5:2–5

The Gadarene was both violent and supernaturally powerful. He lived among the dead, and he continually cried out and mutilated himself. Despite all that, however, when he saw Jesus from afar, he ran and worshiped Him! Jesus immediately commanded, "Come out of the man, unclean spirit!" Then Jesus asked the spirit, "What is your name?" The spirit answered, "My name is Legion; for we are many" (Mark 5:6–9).

At that time, a Roman military legion consisted of six thousand men. That means at least six thousand spirits were troubling this Gadarene. Amazingly, all those thousands of demons could not keep the man from recognizing that there was hope when he looked toward Jesus! They could not prevent him from running and falling down at Jesus' feet in worship and asking for His help. (They could not overpower the man's free will.)

Jesus gave help willingly. At His command to come out of the man, the legion of demonic spirits begged Jesus not to send them out of the country and into torment:

> Now a large herd of swine was feeding there near the mountains. So all the demons begged Him, saying, "Send us to the swine, that we may enter them." And at once Jesus gave them permission. Then the unclean spirits went out and entered the swine (there were about two thousand); and the herd ran violently down the steep place into the sea, and drowned in the sea.
>
> Mark 5:11–13

When the demons went into the pigs, four thousand "deviled hams" ran down that hill! (Every pig contains two hams.) They self-destructed, hurtling off the cliff and into the sea.

102

The devil's ultimate goal for you is always the same: your total destruction. Whether by suicide or by another method that results from sin, your annihilation is his ultimate plan. His plan did not work in regard to the Gadarene, though, who cried out to Jesus for help. It cannot work in regard to you, either. The devil has no ultimate control over your will. Remember, he cannot take you or anyone else to hell if you do not want to go.

The Gadarene demoniac, naked and howling, slashing himself with sharp stones and breaking the iron shackles that bound him, is an extreme example of the horrible effects of the demonic. He is also an example of the tremendous salvation and freedom available in Jesus. After the demons left the man and entered the pigs, the Gadarenes found that the former demoniac was now a completely different person:

> Those who fed the swine fled, and they told it in the city and in the country. And they went out to see what it was that had happened. Then they came to Jesus, and saw the one who had been demon-possessed and had the legion, sitting and clothed and in his right mind. And they were afraid. And those who saw it told them how it happened to him who had been demon-possessed, and about the swine. Then they began to plead with Him to depart from their region.
>
> Mark 5:14–17

Let's look at the twelve things that signaled demon trouble in this man's life and see what we can learn from them. Remember, not all demons are confined to the pages of the Bible or to the unreached wilds of deepest Africa. As we go along, you may recognize some of these signs of demon trouble, which are as prevalent today as they were back in biblical days.

The devil's strategy is to cause trouble everywhere, in every way, every day he can. The Bible says, "Stay alert! Watch out for your great enemy, the devil. He prowls around like a roaring lion, looking for someone to devour" (1 Peter 5:8 NLT). He is always looking for victims to devour. The signs we are about to look at are some outward, visible manifestations of his attacks. They still signal the same demonic activity today that they did in Jesus' time, and they still signal that someone desperately needs to find freedom, in the name of Jesus, from oppression.

Sign 1: Withdrawal from Social Interaction

One of the first signs of demonic activity in a person's life is a withdrawal from social interaction. There is a healthy withdrawal for the purpose of fasting and prayer, but that is done for a short season to draw close to God, and it always results in a desire to return to the fellowship of others. Demonically motivated withdrawal, on the other hand, is severe and continual. The devil always tries to isolate a person from his or her family, friends and local church. People who withdraw to that extent often do so because they do not want to be corrected by those around them.

Mark 5 relates that the Gadarene demoniac withdrew from his family and friends, choosing instead to live among the tombs with only the dead and the demonic for company. The same man's story is also told in Luke 8, which interestingly relates that he was "driven by the demon into the wilderness" (verse 29). Time and again, demonic activity will urge a person toward isolation.

After the Gadarene man was delivered from his oppression, he asked if he could accompany Jesus on His travels. Jesus refused him, telling him instead, "Go home to your own [family and relatives and friends] and bring back word to them of how much the Lord has done for you, and [how He has] had sympathy for you and mercy on you" (Mark 5:19 AMP). Note that the first thing Jesus wanted the man to do once he was free was to restore his personal and social relationships.

God wants you to have a blessed, healthy family life and good, strong friendships. "As iron sharpens iron, so a man sharpens the countenance of his friend," says Proverbs 27:17. Healthy relationships are not only a blessing, they are good for you. Because your relationships are the most valuable things in your life, they are one of the first things the devil attempts to destroy. Consequently, self-imposed isolation is one of the very first signs of demonic activity. People under demonic attack quickly begin to isolate themselves. They break off friendships and family relationships, sometimes in major ways such as separation or divorce in a marriage.

Proverbs 18:1 warns, "A man who isolates himself seeks his own desire; he rages against all wise judgment." Isolating oneself is a means of pulling away from accountability to other people, and it paves the way for an egocentric focus on one's own feelings and desires. It also paves the way for dangerous demonic destruction. A bunch of bananas can illustrate this. We eat a lot of bananas, so Jeanie goes to the store to buy bananas two or three times a week. If she's carrying a bunch of bananas into the house and one breaks off from the rest, guess which banana gets eaten first? The isolated one.

Isolation can be dangerous. Remember, the devil prowls around looking for a victim to devour. When the devil can break people away from their family and friends, he can devour them. When people begin to noticeably isolate themselves, you know that they are entering into dangerous territory. Setting yourself apart from the bunch is like asking to be eaten!

Sign 2: A Tormented Mental State

A second sign of demonic activity is a tormented mental state, wherein a person's mind is constantly bombarded with uncontrollable thoughts. The person may find the thoughts extremely disturbing and would often desperately like to be rid of them, but the thoughts just keep coming. They may involve anxiety or fear; they may be dreams of revenge or may involve violence and murder; they may be perverse thoughts involving illicit or deviant sexual behavior. Whatever their pattern, the person cannot seem to escape or control them.

The Gadarene demoniac experienced such pronounced mental torment that "always, night and day, he was in the mountains and in the tombs, crying out and cutting himself with stones" (Mark 5:5). It is not normal to suffer such pronounced mental distress that you would do anything from self-mutilation to suicide to be free of your thoughts! Yet you will have little difficulty hearing of incidents of self-mutilation today. Many young people have formed the habit of cutting themselves, which they see as a kind of physical release from emotional pain.

The idea that cutting as a form of self-destruction is motivated by an evil spirit can be found in the biblical record. Besides the account of the Gadarene demoniac, 1 Kings 18:28 describes what happened when the prophet Elijah faced the prophets of Baal on Mount Carmel. The false prophets had called on Baal's name from morning until noon but got no response, so in a desperate attempt to capture their god's attention, they "cut themselves, as was their custom, with knives and lances, until the blood gushed out on them." Despite their self-mutilation, the god they worshiped remained silent.

Elijah made no such bloody attempt to reach God. Leviticus 19:28 specifically forbade the Israelites from pagan religious practices such as making cuttings in their flesh. Rather, Elijah touched the heart of God through faith and prayer.

Cutting is rooted in paganism and often occurs because of a tormented mental state. A mind in anguish under that kind of torment still indicates demonic influence today, just as it did in Old Testament times.

Sign 3: Chronic Depression

We learned in chapter 5 that the Bible calls chronic depression—a third sign of demonic activity—"the spirit of heaviness." In Isaiah 61:3, the Hebrew term used for "the spirit of heaviness" carries the meaning of something heavy, dark or smoky. It means to feel weighed down and dark inside.

All of us experience temporary moments of sadness or distress, especially during times of significant loss and grief. The kind of chronic depression I am referring to here, though, means always feeling terrible about yourself and hopeless about life. If you or someone you know constantly feels depressed and negative to that extent, it is a sign of demonic attack.

Note that when the demons left the Gadarene man and entered the herd of swine, the swine were immediately driven to commit suicide. That is the devil's ultimate goal for every person. Your enemy wants you dead, but to him the ultimate victory lies in getting you to destroy yourself. He knows how much God loves you and how precious your life is to your Creator. God redeemed you and bought you with a costly price—the blood of His Son, Jesus. The devil would like to get you to the place, though, where you feel so worthless that you do not see the priceless value God places on you, and you take your own life.

Sign 4: Irrational Fears and Phobias

Demon spirits are all fearful. By that I do not mean they try to engender fear in us, although that is certainly one of their favorite tactics. I mean *they* themselves are frightened. The Bible calls a demon a "spirit of fear" (see 2 Timothy 1:7), and that fear goes both ways. Look at the demons' response to Jesus' presence in the Gadarene's story: "With a shriek, he screamed, 'Why are you interfering with me, Jesus, Son of the Most High

God? In the name of God, I beg you, don't torture me!'" (Mark 5:7 NLT). In another incident during which Jesus expels demons, they also screamed at Him: "Why are you interfering with us, Son of God? Have you come here to torture us before God's appointed time?" (Matthew 8:29 NLT).

The devil and his demons are wildly fearful of the torment that lies ahead for them in the day of judgment. They know they cannot escape their punishment, when they will be cast into the lake of fire (see Revelation 20:10–15). No wonder they are frightened! No wonder they are also bold in their attacks—they know their time is short. They like to spread fear around, causing people who do not aggressively apply God's Word to succumb to irrational fears and phobias of every kind.

Their boldness, however, flees at the thought of their impending doom. They are well aware of what is in store for them. They *should* be afraid, but you do not need to let their fear overflow to you. Believers need suffer no such fears, for we have this assurance from the Lord:

> Love has been perfected among us in this: that we may have boldness in the day of judgment. . . . There is no fear in love; but perfect love casts out fear, because fear involves torment. But he who fears has not been made perfect in love.
>
> 1 John 4:17–18

We need not fear our future in Christ. Unlike Satan and his hordes, we can boldly face the day of judgment. We need not fear the present, either, but misery loves company—the devil and his forces attempt to spread fear everywhere they can. Their goal is to ruin people's lives, and one way they accomplish that is to control people through fear. They deceive people into being frightened of the craziest things.

I asked my assistant one day to find me a list of clinically recognized phobias identified by psychologists, and she came back with fifteen pages of phobias! We are supposedly born with a fear of only two things: falling and loud noises. All other phobias are acquired. You have probably run into people with various phobias; some are quite common, such as nyctophobia (the fear of darkness or night), acrophobia (the fear of heights), cnidophobia (the fear of stings) and arachnophobia (the fear of spiders). But how about some of these? Alektorophobia is the fear of chickens; placophobia, the fear of tombstones; cacophobia, the fear of being ugly; or arachibutyrophobia, the fear of peanut butter sticking to the roof of your mouth. These are all clinically documented fears people suffer from. And if all these big words are getting to you, maybe you are suffering from logophobia, the fear of words!

Did you know some people suffer from the fear of taking a bath (ablutophobia)? Others have motorphobia and amaxophobia, the fear of cars and riding in cars. You should avoid traveling with anyone suffering from these! As a missionary, I once offered a ride to a man who lived far up in the mountains of Mexico. The man had never been in a car before, and he was absolutely petrified! We traveled three hundred miles together, and he vomited all the way.

I think that chionophobia is why so many older people from my part of the country go to Florida for the winter—they fear the snow. And my wife seems to suffer from alliumphobia, the fear of garlic: She is afraid I will eat some. Her fear is not unfounded. One Easter week I had traveled with a group to witness on the beaches in Mexico, which were packed with vacationing city folk. Our resources were meager, so when the big pot of spaghetti meant to be our primary source of nourishment burned, we tried to cover the taste by adding two or three whole *heads* of garlic to the pot. It tasted all right to me, but mysteriously our opportunities for one-on-one witnessing abruptly ended.

When I arrived home Jeanie ran to meet me, only to stop in her tracks ten feet away and gasp. After an hour lying next to me in bed, she declared, "I'm so sorry, honey, but I can't stand the smell emanating from your pores!" She went to sleep elsewhere—the only time in over thirty years of marriage that she left to sleep on the couch.

According to one National Institute of Mental Health statistic, 75 percent of people suffering from a phobia can overcome their fears through cognitive behavioral therapy. The power of God, however, has a much better cure rate than that. More than once the gospels tell us that when the sick were brought to Jesus, He healed *all* who were oppressed of the devil. His cure rate is 100 percent.

God's Word repeatedly says, "Fear not." When you follow God's Word, which says to "Be anxious for nothing, but in everything by prayer and supplication, with thanksgiving, let your requests be made known to God," then "the peace of God, which surpasses all understanding, will guard your hearts and minds through Christ Jesus" (Philippians 4:6–7).

I hope that once you finish reading this book, all traces of satanophobia and demonomania, the fear of the devil and of being possessed by demons, are gone. "For God has not given us a spirit of fear, but of power and of love and of a sound mind" (2 Timothy 1:7). Satan and his demons would like to instill a spirit of fear in you, but that is not God's plan. God's plan is for you to be empowered by His Holy Spirit, filled with His love and in possession of a sound mind untroubled by irrational fears and phobias. Fear is not from God. It is a telltale sign that demonic activity is afoot.

Sign 5: Chronic Restlessness

Before Jesus freed him, the Gadarene demoniac was chronically restless. "Always, night and day, he was in the mountains and in the tombs, crying out and cutting himself" (Mark 5:5). He could not sit still; instead, he constantly had to be on the move.

When a person cannot sit down, relax and enjoy an evening of good fellowship, when he or she constantly has to be on the move, that can signal demonic activity. I am not talking about the high-level energy a child exhibits when fed too much sugar—that is a different kind of restlessness. I am talking about someone in a chronically agitated mental and physical state. Consider the description of the prostitute in Proverbs 7:11–12: "She was loud and rebellious, her feet would not stay at home. At times she was outside, at times in the open square, lurking at every corner."

Granted, a large part of her problem was the illicit sex—one of the fastest ways to usher demonic activity into your life. We will address that again in the next section. But notice she could not be still. She wandered around, discontented to stay at home, and she lurked here and there, full of a driving restlessness.

Jesus said, "Peace I leave with you, My peace I give to you" (John 14:27). Psalm 46:10 says, "Be still, and know that I am God." When you know God's peace, you can sit down, relax and know that He is God. When people are unable to be still and rest in Him, their chronic restlessness may be a sign of demonic influence.

Sign 6: Unclean Desires and Lewd Behavior

Proverbs 7 says the restless prostitute was dressed "with the attire of a harlot" (verse 10). And the Luke 8 version of the demoniac's tale says the Gadarene man "wore no clothes" (verse 27). Lewd behavior, including dressing immodestly, is a serious sign of demonic activity. No doubt that is an unpopular statement in today's society, where immodest dress and lewd behavior once considered sinful are now considered normal. In fact, a person who does not consider lewdness normal and acceptable is now branded a prude, and being a prude is viewed as a much bigger crime these days than any indecency.

Along the same lines, people who do not consider the gay lifestyle normal are also branded intolerant and politically incorrect. Yet Romans 1:26–27 clearly states that women desiring women and men desiring men is unnatural and indecent. There is nothing normal about being gay—it is a demonically motivated lifestyle with demonically devastating results. I know that is not a popular statement, but it is true.

You need to know that I am not mad at gay people. Just as God hates sin but loves every sinner, I feel compassion toward gay people, though the gay lifestyle is sinful. I want to see them saved, healed and delivered; I want God's grace and mercy to flow to them so they can get right with God and have hearts full of joy, peace and purpose. Until that happens, they are trapped in twisted thinking and in danger from the devil.

In Scripture, we were forewarned of such shifts in thought, in which right becomes wrong and wrong becomes right: "But know this, that in the last days perilous times will come: For men will be lovers of themselves . . . lovers of pleasure rather than lovers of God" (2 Timothy 3:1–2, 4). The word *perilous* in that passage means "dangerous." The shift into a new worldview that glorifies illicit sex is a dangerous thing.

I find it interesting that in 1 Corinthians 6, in which Paul talks about illicit sexual behavior, he asks several times, "Do you not know?"—as if he assumed *anyone* should know the dangers involved. "Do you not know that he who is joined to a harlot is one body with her?" he asks. "For 'the two,' He [the Lord] says, 'shall become one flesh'" (verse 16). "Flee sexual immorality," Paul continues. "Every sin that a man does is outside the body, but he who commits sexual immorality sins against his own body" (verse 18).

The Greek word Paul uses for "body" is *soma*, and it carries a second meaning: "slave." When people engage in illicit sex, not only do they become one body, they become one slave. How?

Picture it this way: As two people become one body, a bridge forms in the spirit world between them. Every spirit that is in one person can cross over that bridge built by physical intimacy and influence the other person. If the spirits are demonic, they now enslave not just one person, but both.

Let me illustrate with an example. I knew of a young lady, a cheerleader and senior in high school, who had a wonderful testimony about being saved. She kept herself pure and said she had no desire, no temptation whatsoever, to misuse drugs and alcohol. She became involved with a young man three or four years older than she was and found out he was not saved. Because she had developed strong feelings for him, she decided to continue their relationship. She determined to win him to the Lord.

Missionary dating is never a good idea. The Bible says, "Do not be unequally yoked together with unbelievers. For what fellowship has righteousness with lawlessness? And what communion has light with darkness?" (2 Corinthians 6:14). If you are a Christian, you belong to God, and you have no right to date or consider marrying someone who does not belong to God. God warns us to steer clear of such compromising situations.

This young lady did not heed the Bible's warning. She was in love, and soon the guy pressured her to compromise her morals. Every time they went out, he would say, "If you love me, you'll sleep with me. . . . If you love me, you'll sleep with me." Besides the immoral behavior he was advocating, he was already an alcoholic at the age of 22. He was also addicted to cocaine. This young lady was completely unaware of it, for he had carefully hidden his worst vices from her.

One night these two attended a party together. Again he told her he loved her, and he begged, "Sleep with me! If you love me, you'll sleep with me." She finally gave in to his pleading, sure that they were on their way to marriage and a long, happy life together. A mere six weeks later, *she* was addicted to cocaine and was well on her way to becoming an alcoholic. Her missionary dating had not been successful. She wound up more miserable than she had ever been in her life.

What happened? She became one *soma*, one body, with the troubled young man—and also one slave with him to his addictions. The demonic influences that held sway over his life now had full access to her life, and they came in full force. They easily crossed the spiritual bridge directly from him to her.

Why did it not happen the other way around, so that the godly spiritual influences in this young lady crossed over and she won the unbelieving young man to the Lord? Think about which is easier: for you to pull someone up on a platform with you, or for them to pull you down. She tried to pull him up to her spiritual level, but he was not cooperating. He was more interested in pulling her down instead. "Do not be misled," 1 Corinthians 15:33 warns. "Bad company corrupts good character" (NIV). If you add pure water to muddy water, which one does the resulting mixture look more like?

It is one thing to evangelize from a position outside an unbeliever's life but quite another to missionary-date from the inside, mixing your Christian lifestyle with someone else's ungodly lifestyle. While your date's muddy waters may indeed become somewhat cleaner due to your influence, your pure water is also going to be muddied in the process. You will likely be the one most noticeably affected by being unequally yoked, not the unbelieving person. It has happened time and time again.

Paul simply assumed the people of his time knew that mixing pure and muddy waters, morally speaking, could not possibly result in a clean life. I guarantee that our society will not automatically teach such things; you will not know them unless you have been taught them from the Bible. Despite AIDS and the rampant spread of sexually transmitted diseases even among our youth, our society is totally ignorant of these principles. In its ignorance it glorifies illicit sex, but make no mistake—unclean desires and lewd or immodest behavior are strong indicators of demonic activity, and they will destroy a person's life.

Sign 7: Addictive and Compulsive Behaviors

People who feel driven to repeat odd or destructive actions over and over are suffering from addictive or compulsive behavior problems. Psychologists sometimes refer to these problems as disorders, but many are actually demonic in origin. Scripture says of the Gadarene man, whose behavior was certainly both odd and destructive, that he "was driven by the demon" (Luke 8:29). Such is still the case with many people today.

Some obvious examples of such behavior include the abuse of alcohol and drugs, uncontrollable gambling and involvement in illicit sex or pornography. That is the short list, but any behavior that captures someone so that they cannot seem to break away from it under their own power falls into this category.

One thing that happens when people repent and come to know God's truth is that they "come to their senses and escape the snare of the devil, having been taken captive by him to do his will" (2 Timothy 2:26). After they are no longer the devil's captives, the Spirit of God will lead and guide them—but never does the Holy Spirit force them. God always allows people the right to exercise their free will and make choices.

The devil, however, operates quite differently. He wants to take people prisoners of war and drive them to do *his* will. He wants people's wills to become passive, so that the more he tempts them in certain areas, the more they fall. His goal is that finally they will exert no resistance. The more they give in to temptation, the less willpower remains to stand up and "Just say no!" Then the devil drives them into addictive and compulsive behaviors they cannot seem to stop, which are definite signs of demonic subterfuge.

Sign 8: Uncontrollable Rage

The Gadarene demoniac gave vent to such uncontrollable rage that, no doubt for their own safety, the townspeople captured him and kept him bound with chains—at least that was their plan. Mark 5:4 (NIV) says they had to bind him again and again, "for he had often been chained hand and foot, but he tore the chains apart and broke the irons on his feet." When he was subdued, the townspeople would bind him with chains and irons, but whenever the demonic spirit in him was manifesting itself, he would display superhuman strength and break his bonds.

Any time someone flies off the handle repeatedly, letting it all go in uncontrollable rage, it signals demonic manifestation. Ecclesiastes 7:9 says, "Anger rests in the bosom of fools." Ephesians 4:26–27 warns, "'Don't sin by letting anger control you.' Don't let the sun go down while you are still angry, for anger gives a foothold to the devil" (NLT). People who bottle up anger on the inside until the pressure is so intense that it explodes uncontrollably on the outside have given the devil an inroad. Their uncontrollable rage signals demonic activity in their lives.

Sign 9: Violent Behavior

The Gadarene did not break off his chains and shackles under his own power. His supernatural violence was demonically motivated. The same is true of extremely violent behavior today. We have seen numerous horrific school shootings in recent years; such extreme violence is demonic.

Violence does not have to display supernatural strength to be demonic, of course. When King Saul was under the influence of an evil or distressing spirit, he attempted to pin David to the wall with a spear while David was playing music on the harp for him. Another time, Saul tried to kill his own son and heir, Jonathan, with a spear. Throwing a spear does not require supernatural strength, but Saul's violence against David and Jonathan was nonetheless supernaturally motivated (see 1 Samuel 19:9–10; 20:30–33).

Times may come when violence is necessary in self-defense or in defense of one's family or one's country, but unwarranted and extreme violence is a sign of demonic activity.

Sign 10: A Fixation on Death and the Occult

The Gadarene demoniac lived in the tombs, among the dead—not a good place to live! And when the legion of spirits came out of him, the swine they entered ran down the hill and committed suicide.

God put inside us a natural aversion to death, so when people become fixated on death, it signifies demonic activity. So does a fixation on the occult and occult symbols.

Not many of us from Western cultures know much about the occult. We may not really think about what we bring into our houses as decoration, but God thinks a lot about it because certain things can attract demonic activity. In Deuteronomy 7:26, God instructs, "Do not bring any detestable objects into your home, for then you will be destroyed, just like them. You must utterly detest such things, for they are set apart for destruction" (NLT).

The detestable objects this verse refers to were idols or the silver and gold out of which the idols were made. In essence, though, detestable objects, or "abominations," as some translations call them, can mean any objects having to do with another god or with spiritual powers other than God Himself. Copies of idols—for example, little Buddhas and the like—can attract demonic activity. So can things such as what people call "the eye of God," along with pentagrams and other symbols with known connections to the occult. God warns us not to bring such things into our possession, lest we be set apart for destruction just as they are.

Howard Carter once related an example of this. Carter was a great Bible teacher and author who served as chairman of the Assemblies of God in Great Britain for a number of years. For 27 years he was also the principal of the first Pentecostal Bible school in Europe, known as the Hampstead Bible School. The school trained evangelists, pastors and teachers, who were sent to mission fields all over the world to spread the Gospel. One time an alumnus missionary visited the school after serving in India. While on the mission field, he had bought a big brass cobra, and he gave it to Carter. Carter thought, *I want our students to have a vision for reaching the world, and this is a good reminder of India—I'm going to put it in the back of my classroom.*

Carter was known as a dynamic speaker, but the day after he placed that brass cobra in his classroom, something happened that he did not recall ever happening to him before. A large number of his students fell asleep while he was speaking. Every day after that, many students continued to fall asleep during his lectures. Carter prayed about their sudden inattentiveness and asked the Lord, *What's going on?*

You may already know that many people in India worship the cobra. The Lord brought the brass cobra to Carter's mind, and he felt like the Lord said, *Get rid of it!* Carter did not say anything to anyone, but he took the cobra out of his classroom, took it behind the school, dug a six-foot hole, threw it in and buried it. The next day not one student fell asleep while he was speaking, and as long as he taught in the Bible school, he never had another student fall asleep in class.

Symbols of idol worship and the occult draw demonic activity. We must refuse them entry into our homes and lives or else suffer the destructive results.

Sign 11: Suicidal Thoughts

Demonic forces extinguish a person's desire to live, which makes sense when you consider all the other negative effects their presence brings: social withdrawal, a tormented mind, chronic depression, irrational fears and phobias, chronic restlessness, unclean desires and lewd behavior, addictive and compulsive behaviors, uncontrollable rage, violent behaviors and a fixation on death and the occult. All these things drive a person toward self-destruction.

A person may start by showing signs of a problem in only one or two of these areas, but before long he or she can become like the Gadarene, living a miserable existence, desperate enough to do *anything* to stop the pain. It is only a small step from there to the devil's ultimate goal for him or her, suicide.

The devil's number-one purpose is to steal from, kill and utterly destroy people. He considers it a monumental victory to get someone to commit suicide. As soon as his demonic forces left the Gadarene and entered the swine, all two thousand pigs ran off a cliff to their deaths. He would like to see all of us do the same.

Forces that cause someone to focus on death, to long for it and to suffer from suicidal thoughts, are wholly satanic. God meant for each of us to have life, and have it abundantly (see John 10:10).

Sign 12: Absolute Helplessness

Sometimes people reach the point of absolute helplessness. They have done all they know how to do to escape the things that bind them. They have tried and tried to change, they have read every self-help book, they have asked for advice, maybe even gone to counseling, but despite all efforts, nothing changes. That is a sign of demonic sabotage.

"Neither could anyone tame him," Mark 5:4 says of the Gadarene. No one could help the man—and he surely was not able to help himself. He was right where the devil wanted him—right where the devil wants us all. He was a helpless, hopeless case.

There is only one cure for the kind of absolute helplessness and hopelessness brought on by the demonic, and the Gadarene man knew the cure when he saw it—the moment he saw Jesus step ashore in his country. A whole legion of demons could not stop the Gadarene from crying out to Jesus for mercy and help then, and the same is true for anyone afflicted by demon trouble today.

Twelve Signs, One Cure

"You who seek God . . . let your hearts revive and live!" Psalm 69 declares. "For the Lord hears the poor and needy and despises not His prisoners (His miserable and wounded ones)" (verses 32–33 AMP).

Now that we have uncovered a dozen signs of demon trouble, we know what the devil and his hordes can do. They are out to steal from, kill and destroy anyone who does not resist them, who allows them a foothold or who is ignorant of their devices. Anyone who cries out to the Lord for help, though, as the Gadarene man did, will find Him answering in their desperate time of need. After all, Jesus came to preach, to heal and to set the captives free. He announced,

The Spirit of the Sovereign LORD is on me, because the LORD has anointed me to proclaim good news to the poor. He has sent me to bind up the brokenhearted, to proclaim *freedom for the captives* and *release from darkness for the prisoners*.

Isaiah 61:1 NIV (italics added)

In the chapter that follows, we will learn about what Jesus did to counteract the demonic realm's terrible effect on people's lives. We will examine a dozen ways to disarm the devil, and we will take up the weapons He provided for us—powerful, invincible weapons with which we can demonstrate Satan's defeat.

8

Jesus the Deliverer

Disarming the Devil

Having disarmed principalities and powers, He made a public spectacle of them, triumphing over them in it [the cross].

Colossians 2:15

Had you been born in the world of ancient Rome, you might have beheld the spectacle of the Roman Triumph once or twice in your lifetime. The Roman Triumph was a civil and religious ceremony that publicly honored a victorious military commander returning from battle. It was the highest honor Rome could bestow on a leader, and it included a parade so spectacular that scenes from a Triumph were often permanently etched into stone monuments afterward.

The commander, or *triumphator*, was dressed in a royal purple tunic and rode in a magnificent gilded chariot pulled by two white horses. Over his head, a slave held a laurel wreath, while whispering continuously in his ear, "*Memento mori*"—"Remember thou art mortal." So great were the accolades a triumphator received on the day of his Triumph that the Romans felt he must be reminded he was not divine!

Paving the way for the triumphator's chariot were the spoils of war—cartloads of gold and priceless treasures plundered from the enemy and carried home to enrich Rome. Carvings of Titus' Triumph after the sack of Jerusalem, for example, display a seven-branched menorah among the spoils to signify his victory over the Jews. Preceding the spoils of war, the chiefs, and preferably the king, of a vanquished country would stumble along, dazed and bound in chains. Roman generals often made a point of capturing their opponents alive, intending to publicly ridicule them by parading them in a Roman Triumph. (Afterward the opponents were usually executed, of course.) So degrading was it to be thus paraded as a vanquished foe of Rome that Egypt's Queen Cleopatra chose to commit suicide rather than suffer the humiliation of Octavian's Triumph.

Roman Triumphs were held over a period of a thousand years, so the people of Jesus' time—Roman or not, Jewish or Gentile, young or old—were all familiar with the ceremony. They well understood the depth and breadth a victory must have to warrant the celebration of a Triumph for the commander. They also understood the utter depth of defeat an enemy of Rome would suffer in being subjected to such a spectacle. That is why, when Paul penned Colossians 2:15, he knew people of all ages, near and far, would understand the implication of his words. He knew his imagery would paint a mental picture for his readers of the glorious, unparalleled victory Jesus the Deliverer wrought over our enemy, the devil.

Note again the words with which Paul described Jesus' victory: *Having disarmed principalities and powers*—Jesus stripped the dark kingdom's ruler and his forces of their weapons. Then, *He made a public spectacle of them*, seizing the keys to death and hell (Revelation 1:18), so that we can now say, "O death, where is thy sting? O grave, where is thy victory?" (1 Corinthians 15:55 KJV). *Triumphing over them* in the cross, Jesus wrested away the victory the devil had hoped to achieve, so that, rather than serving as a symbol of shame for the Son of God, the cross now stands as a symbol of shame for the devil. The cross was the battlefield on which Satan was wholly defeated. There Jesus the Deliverer triumphed over Satan once and for all and then exclaimed, "It is finished!" (John 19:30).

Also note that at the end of the ages Satan is bound in chains and comes to a terrible end, just like the vanquished enemies of Rome. In Revelation 20 John relates,

> I saw an Angel descending out of Heaven. He carried the key to the Abyss and a chain—a huge chain. He grabbed the Dragon, that old Snake—the very Devil, Satan himself!—chained him up for a thousand years, dumped him into the Abyss, slammed it shut and sealed it tight. No more trouble out of him . . .
>
> Verses 1–3 MESSAGE

No More Trouble

We are about to examine a number of spiritual weapons Jesus our Deliverer provided for us through His death, burial, resurrection and ascension. With them He disarmed the devil—and He has given you and me authority to do the same! If you will employ these powerful weapons of warfare that Jesus provided, you, too, can begin to experience no more trouble out of the devil.

Satan will certainly continue to tempt, lay traps and plot trouble, but you are now delivered from the enemy's kingdom. After all, "The reason the Son of God was made manifest (visible) was to undo (destroy, loosen, and dissolve) the works the devil [has done]" (1 John 3:8 AMP). That verse paints a marvelous mental picture of what happens as you pick up and wield the mighty weapons of your warfare. The works the devil wrought in your life, the effects his interference has had up until now, will be broken off you. They were destroyed by your Deliverer. Jesus gave Himself for you and me so that He "might bring to nought and make of no effect" the devil (Hebrews 2:14 AMP).

Merriam-Webster's dictionary defines *nought* as "nothing"— none, zero, literally of no effect. That is how much God wants the devil to affect your life: zero, or not at all. Though I like thinking about all the things the devil cannot do, I am even more excited by all the ways Jesus has provided for us to demonstrate Satan's defeat!

Jesus did not defeat the devil just to prove that He could. He defeated him for us so we might reap the benefits, having at our disposal everything we need to disarm the devil.

> For though we walk (live) in the flesh, we are not carrying on our warfare according to the flesh and using mere human weapons. For the weapons of our warfare are not physical [weapons of flesh and blood], but they are mighty before God for the over-throw and destruction of strongholds.
>
> 2 Corinthians 10:3–4 AMP

Let's familiarize ourselves with the weapons of our warfare.

Take Authority in the Name of Jesus

The first and foremost weapon we can wield to demonstrate Satan's defeat is our authority in Jesus' name. In using His name, Jesus gave us the power of attorney, so to speak: "Most assuredly, I say to you, whatever you ask the Father in My name He will give you. Until now you have asked nothing in My name. Ask, and you will receive, that your joy may be full" (John 16:23–24).

Power of attorney is a legal instrument authorizing one person to act as an agent of another, who is the grantor. When Jeanie and I were missionaries in Mexico, I granted my brother-in-law power of attorney. He could sign my name to legal documents, take money out of my bank account and do all sorts of things as if I were there to do them myself.

Spiritually speaking, Jesus is the grantor. He has authorized each child of God to act as His agent on this earth. We are His representatives, enforcing what legally belongs to us through His death, burial and resurrection.

Jesus told us in Matthew 16:19, "I will give you the keys of the kingdom of heaven, and whatever you bind on earth will be bound in heaven, and whatever you loose on earth will be loosed in heaven." The authority Adam yielded to Satan at the Fall has been restored to us. When Adam fell, he lost his dominion and Satan became the god (small g) of this world. But Jesus, in His death, burial and resurrection, won that authority back. "All authority has been given to Me in heaven and on earth," Jesus declared to his disciples. "Go therefore and make disciples of all the nations" (Matthew 28:18–19). The first thing Jesus did when He won back that authority was restore it to you and me—with this authority we can go forth in His name, fulfilling the Great Commission. Whether we have been Christians for forty minutes or forty years, we now have full authority in Jesus' name.

Jesus handed us His keys to the Kingdom. Imagine what you could do if I handed you my keys. Anywhere I go—my home, my office, my cabin—you could enter easily. Anything I own that requires a key—my car, my boat, my lawn tractor—you could start easily. My keys do not care whose hands they are in, yours or mine; if I give them to you, they work as well for you as for me. They give you access to anything I own. All I have is now at your disposal.

Likewise, all Jesus has is now at your disposal. One of the keys He gave us is His name, and His name in your mouth works the same for you as it does for any other believer. You need not be a famous pastor or evangelist to use Jesus' name and get results. His name opens the door to God's blessings and shuts the door to the devil. But you have to *use* it—wield it as the weapon that it is.

If you stand outside my car in the pouring rain, holding my car keys but never unlocking the door, you will not get anywhere (except wet). The same thing happens spiritually. Many believers have heard Scriptures about Jesus' name over and over, how it is above all names and how signs and wonders follow those who believe in His name. They honor His name in their hearts, but they do not use it as a key to enforce Satan's defeat in the midst of a storm or trial. They do not take their God-given authority and speak that name to bind and to loose. Because they do not invoke their power of attorney and *use* the name of Jesus, they remain unable to enter into the victory Jesus purchased for them at the cross.

Realize that you cannot "think" the name of Jesus at the devil and his cronies. We learned earlier that they are not omniscient, omnipotent or omni-anything—this means they are not all-knowing or all-powerful, and they *do not know* what you are thinking! You have to verbally take authority over them in the name of Jesus. Tell them out loud, "In Jesus' name I bind you and your interference off [the specific situation]!"

"If you have faith as a mustard seed," Jesus said, "you will *say* to this mountain, 'Move from here to there,' and it will move; and nothing will be impossible for you" (Matthew 17:20, italics added). If you have faith in His name, you will *say*, you will *speak*. You will talk to spiritual mountains or storms, and nothing will be impossible for you.

At this point some of you may be thinking, *I do believe in Jesus, but it doesn't work the way you say it should for me.*

Realize there is a difference between believing in Jesus and believing in His name. Even as a Christian, you can believe in Jesus without believing in His name—and thus doing without the benefits that come with believing in His name. The importance of believing in His name is described in 1 John 3:23: "And this is his [God the Father's] commandment: We must believe *in the name* of his Son, Jesus Christ, and love one another, just as he commanded us" (NLT, italics added).

What does that mean? What is the difference? Many people who believe in Jesus but not necessarily in His name have come to me and said, "Pastor, if only Jesus would come down and touch me, I know I would be healed! If only He would appear to me just for a minute and lay His hand on my head, everything would be all right." That wish sounds spiritual, but it is not. Right now Jesus is seated at the right hand of the Father in heaven, and that is where He will stay until His enemies are made His footstool (see Hebrews 10:12–13). He ascended into heaven, but He left us *His name*. People who do not recognize it for the weapon it is are praying down here, *Jesus, come and heal me; Jesus, come and help me; Jesus, the devil's after me!* Meanwhile, up in heaven, God the Father is answering, "My child, Jesus already did His part—now *you* do something in His name!"

As we saw earlier in Philippians 2:10, "at the name of Jesus every knee should bow, in heaven and on earth and under the earth" (NLT). Everything that has a name (cancer, depression, poverty or anything else) has to bow to the name of Jesus. His name is above all names. The book of Acts indicates that for the first several years after the resurrection, the disciples preached almost exclusively on the name of Jesus. Enormous power resides in Jesus' name, and He does not need to be physically present for that power to be effective.

It is no different than if I wrote you a $1,000 check. Once I signed it, you would know what to do next! You would not beg me to come down to the bank personally to help you cash it. With my signature on it, you would confidently hand it to the cashier and get the money.

The same holds true with Jesus' name. Jesus does not need to make a flesh-and-blood appearance for you to use His name and receive its powerful benefits. Satan and demon forces *must* recognize the authority in Jesus' name, whether it is Jesus standing against them or you standing there using His name.

Conversely, when people do not recognize the authority they have in Jesus' name, neither will the devil recognize it in their lives. Acts 19 relates an incident when some itinerant Jewish exorcists, imitating the apostle Paul, took it upon themselves to call on the name of Jesus over those who were possessed by evil spirits. Seven sons of Sceva, a Jewish chief priest, told a demon spirit, "We exorcise you by the Jesus whom Paul preaches" (verse 13).

Those boys may have thought their religious position as sons of the chief priest gave them authority to use Jesus' name, but it did not! They did not know Jesus, had not made Him their Lord and were not His disciples. Hence the evil spirit's retort: "I know Jesus and I've heard of Paul, but who are you?" Then it caused its host, in the words of *The Message*, to go "berserk"—the man "jumped the exorcists, beat them up, and tore off their clothes. Naked and bloody, they got away as best they could" (verses 15–16).

That demon knew Jesus all right, and it had heard about Paul. It did not, however, recognize anything in those young men that gave them the authority to use Jesus' name. How about you? Has your name appeared on the list of those who belong to Jesus, those who are saved and dangerous to the devil?

Jesus must be your Lord for you to have power of attorney to represent Him. When you *belong* to Jesus, then the power in

His name belongs to you. Once you are saved and have authority to use His name, *not* using it is like throwing that $1,000 check I gave you into the trash without ever trying to cash it at the bank, because you are not convinced of the power of my name on the signature line. What a waste.

Let's not waste the most magnificent weapon of our warfare, dropping it by the wayside while we beg Jesus to come *do* something about the devil. Jesus already defeated him. Let's start using the authority we have in His name and demonstrate that defeat.

Know the Truth

"Jesus said to those Jews who had believed in Him, If you abide in My word [hold fast to My teachings and live in accordance with them], you are truly My disciples. And you will know the Truth, and the Truth will set you free" (John 8:31–32 AMP).

It is not the truth that frees a person, but *knowing* the Truth and *practicing* it. You must put into practice your knowledge of the truth about your authority over your defeated enemy, the devil. To know goes beyond mental assent. Merriam-Webster also defines the verb *know* as "to have experience of" and "to have a practical understanding of." In any area, when you practically apply what knowledge you have to your everyday experiences, you get results.

When Jesus said, "you will know the truth," the word He used for *know* also meant "to have absolute knowledge of" and "to be resolved to speak in agreement." If you will abide in that awesome Word of God, practice its truths and speak in agreement with it, you will discover freedom. To *know* the truth in God's Word—know it in the ways we have talked about here—is a powerful weapon with which we can resist the enemy.

131

Identify the Enemy

We cannot successfully oppose an enemy whom we have not identified. The importance of identifying our enemy is why we examined the biography of the devil in chapter 2. Because the devil is our bitter personal adversary, Peter urged us, "Stay alert! Watch out for your great enemy, the devil. He prowls around like a roaring lion, looking for someone to devour" (1 Peter 5:8 NLT). The devil may prowl like a roaring lion, but if you have identified him as your defeated enemy, he can roar until he is hoarse—while you enjoy the victory.

Like a lion, the devil must *look* for his victims. Have you seen nature documentaries about lions on the prowl? They do not go after the strongest or fastest animals in a herd; they go after the weaklings. The weak, the slow, the sick become their victims. So it is with the devil. He must look for those who are hindered because they do not know they have authority over him. Those who are weak in their resistance, who are slow to recognize his tricks or who open the door through sin become his prey.

Often Christians are caught off guard because they do not realize they are in the middle of a spiritual war and do not identify their enemy. Or they try for a truce, thinking, *If I leave the devil alone, he'll leave me alone.* That is a failing strategy. If you hide your head in the sand and act like there is no battle, the devil will devour you. If you identify your enemy, familiarize yourself with his tactics and wield the weapons Jesus provided, you will gain the victory.

Resist, Resist, Resist

After Peter warned us that the devil prowls around like a roaring lion, he went on to say, "Resist him, steadfast in the faith" (1 Peter 5:9). Or, as another translation puts it, "Stand firm against him" (NLT). How do we resist? We stand up and boldly declare, "No, Satan—not in my life you don't. I'm a child of the King! Be gone in Jesus' name!" Using our authority in Jesus' name is our first line of resistance against the devil.

Nowhere in the Bible does it say, "If the devil is after you, pray." It does say, "Resist him, steadfast in the faith" (1 Peter 5:9), and "Submit to God. Resist the devil and he will flee from you" (James 4:7). When he comes at you with his destruction, come back at him with God's Word. As I said earlier, the last time the devil fled from you is the last time you resisted him. Resist with everything in you—your words, your choices, your actions. If you do not resist, he will not flee and you cannot experience victory.

When Israel sent twelve spies into the Promised Land, the spies found the land flowing with milk and honey. They brought back some of its amazing fruits for the people—they had cut from a grapevine one cluster of grapes so big that the Bible says they carried it "between two of them on a pole" (Numbers 13:23). Imagine one cluster of grapes taking two full-grown men to carry it. Those grapes are not the kind I buy at the grocery store!

Despite the big, bountiful fruit, though, there was a problem in the Promised Land: "We went to the land where you sent us," the spies reported. "It truly flows with milk and honey, and this is its fruit. Nevertheless the people who dwell in the land are strong; the cities are fortified and very large; moreover we saw the descendants of Anak [giants] there" (Numbers 13:27–28). Not at all what the Israelites had hoped for. Of the twelve spies, only Caleb and Joshua argued for going in and taking the Promised Land. Ten spies dissented, and all the people with them—though God had already given them possession of it.

Many Christians act like those dissenters, wanting God's blessings to simply fall down on them like ripe cherries from a tree. "Rain down the blessings, Lord, we're ready to receive," they pray—so long as possessing those blessings does not take any effort on their part. If you read in Ephesians 6:12 (KJV), "We wrestle not," and take that to mean, "Yep, that's right—we wrestle not," sit on your couch, watch talk shows and eat Twinkies, you cannot expect to live a victorious Christian life. You have to finish the rest of the verse: "We wrestle not against flesh and blood, but against principalities, against powers, against the rulers of the darkness of this world, against spiritual wickedness in high places." All around you a battle is going on in the spiritual realm, and you are either taking ground or giving it—there is no neutral zone.

When the Israelites wanted to enter the Promised Land, they had to go in and *take* it. The same is true of you and me. If we want to live a victorious Christian life in the Kingdom, we have to take possession of it. We need to stand up to some giants, tear down some strongholds and resist the devil. The Israelites got to looking at the giants instead of God's promises, and as a result they wanted to run from the battle. We need to keep our eyes on the grapes—the benefits and blessings of our Promised Land—and resist until the devil flees.

Understand You Were Transferred at Salvation

To stand victorious and demonstrate Satan's defeat, you need to understand that when you accepted Jesus as Lord and were saved, your transfer went through. That is, God rescued you from the kingdom of darkness and gave you a new address in His own Kingdom. "[The Father] has delivered and drawn us to Himself out of the control and the dominion of darkness and has transferred us into the kingdom of the Son of His love," says Colossians 1:13 (AMP).

Not only have you been transferred, you have also been qualified. Colossians 1:12 tells us to be "giving thanks to the Father who has qualified us to be partakers of the inheritance of the saints in the light." God did not transfer and qualify us because we are perfect; He saved us in spite of ourselves and qualified us through the blood of His Son. For what did He qualify us? To be partakers of—to take part in—the inheritance of the saints.

Suppose a rich relative dies and leaves you something in his or her will. When you are notified about the reading of the will, you make sure you show up to receive what is bequeathed to you. The Word of God is like such a notice. It notifies you that your older brother, Jesus Christ, died and left you an inheritance that includes all the blessings of His Kingdom.

God fully qualified you to receive your Kingdom inheritance. The only one contesting the will is the devil, who constantly attempts to keep you from receiving all the benefits of your salvation—never mind that it is all down on paper, in black and white, with God's seal upon His Word.

The devil is a swindler. He will continue to steal from you and destroy your life if you let him. You are no longer a sorry citizen of Satan's kingdom, though, and he has no legal right to put anything on you. Any time he tries to, he is trespassing on God's property. That is why you must exercise your power of attorney in Jesus' name and stand up to the devil. Tell him, "No you don't! I've been transferred, I've moved, and that evil you have planned for me is *not* part of my inheritance. It doesn't belong in the new Kingdom I'm living in—take it back where it came from. Be gone in Jesus' name!"

The court of heaven has declared Satan's former legal claims on you null and void—his control over you is now revoked. You still live in a world where he is god (small g), but you are not of it—you are a citizen of a better Kingdom. "Now, therefore, you are no longer strangers and foreigners, but fellow citizens with the saints and members of the household of God" (Ephesians 2:19). Or, as *The Message* translation so beautifully says,

"You're no longer wandering exiles. *This kingdom of faith is now your home country.* You're no longer strangers or outsiders. You belong here, *with as much right* to the name Christian as anyone" (italics added).

Your move from one kingdom to another is in itself a powerful weapon. With your transfer, Satan's rights over you have been revoked and your rights as an heir of God's Kingdom have been restored. You now reside in the best neighborhood there is, the Kingdom of God, and you can enjoy all the benefits of your new place of residence. The next section takes a closer look at the benefits you enjoy and the curses you have escaped.

Know You Are Blessed, Not Cursed

It is important to know what you have been transferred away from. That way, when the devil shows up at your door to deliver some package from his kingdom of darkness, you will know better than to sign for it. Remember that knowledge of the enemy is power to disarm him. You can use this knowledge as a weapon to protect yourself.

What does the devil no longer have the right to put on you? "Christ has redeemed us from the curse of the law, having become a curse for us (for it is written, 'Cursed is everyone who hangs on a tree [is crucified]')" (Galatians 3:13). Anything under the curse of the Law does not belong in your life.

The curse of the Law is found in Deuteronomy 28. Those living in the kingdom of darkness, far from God, are cursed in the city and cursed in the country (verse 16). Their produce is meager physically, materially and financially (verses 17–18). They are cursed coming and going; they are confused and disillusioned; they suffer mental and emotional difficulties (verses 19–20). Disease, famine and defeat are rampant in their lives (verses 21–29). They sow much but reap little; their personal relationships suffer; their hearts and their health break (verses 30 to the end). The kingdom of darkness is a terrible place to reside!

Here is a helpful aside on your health: Deuteronomy 28:60–61 warns that the curse includes all the diseases mentioned in the Book (the Bible) and all the diseases not mentioned. If you include all the sicknesses named in the Bible and all the sicknesses not named, are there any others? Of course not. If you have been redeemed from the curse of the Law, how many diseases have you been delivered from? Right—all of them. You do not need to accept any package Satan tries to deliver that affects your physical, mental, emotional or spiritual health.

The curse of the Law belongs in the kingdom of darkness, but your new position is in the Kingdom of God's beloved Son, where you have been qualified for your share in the inheritance. In Psalm 103, David called your inheritance "benefits":

> Bless the LORD, O my soul, and forget not all His benefits: Who forgives all your iniquities, who heals all your diseases, who redeems your life from destruction, who crowns you with loving-kindness and tender mercies, who satisfies your mouth with good things, so that your youth is renewed like the eagle's.
>
> Psalm 103:2–5

That is the short list of your blessings. Bible scholars count seven thousand promises in the Bible; Peter called them "exceedingly great and precious promises" (2 Peter 1:4). Each promise is "yes and amen" for you—"No matter how many promises God has made, they are 'Yes' in Christ. And so through him the 'Amen' is spoken by us to the glory of God" (2 Corinthians 1:20 NIV). Those promises are your share in the inheritance of the saints.

The choice between blessings and curses is as simple as the choice to be saved and transfer your allegiance from the kingdom of darkness to the Kingdom of God's beloved Son. We talked in chapter 4 about how the devil cannot violate your free will. God gives you the right to choose your place of citizenship. In Deuteronomy 30:19–20, God presents you with your options:

> I call heaven and earth as witnesses today against you, that I have set before you life and death, blessing and cursing; therefore choose life, that both you and your descendants may live; that you may love the LORD your God, that you may obey His voice, and that you may cling to Him, for He is your life and the length of your days.

In effect God gives you a multiple-choice test: "You must choose: Choice A—life and blessing. Choice B—death and curses." Then God tells you the answer to His test in advance: "Choose life, that you and your descendants might live."

It does not take much studying to pass that test. Our loving heavenly Father has provided us with the answers to escaping the devil's curses and securing life, health and blessings in advance.

Put On Righteousness

To demonstrate Satan's defeat, you must know that you are righteous. People with religious mind-sets put the brakes on when they hear that they can be righteous. It is a religious spirit that always judges and condemns people and makes them feel they cannot be good enough for God. Thoughts such as "You'll never measure up," "Your past is too awful" or "God can't forgive and use someone like you" would never come from the Holy Spirit, who always speaks to convince you of your right standing with God *in Christ*.

I remember attending church with one young lady whom I dated before I met my wife and before I met Jesus. Her minister would say something, and the congregants would respond, "I'm a sinner." Then he would say something else, and again everyone would respond, "I'm a sinner." This went on for several minutes, and every time we responded, "I'm a sinner," I felt lower and lower. I walked out of that church feeling farther than ever from God, not closer to Him. A religious spirit does that to people, making them feel condemned, hopeless and distant from God.

God's Word does state that, according to the Law, "There is no one righteous, not even one. . . . No one will be declared righteous in God's sight by the works of the law" (Romans 3:10, 20 NIV). However, it goes on to say,

> But now apart from the law the righteousness of God has been made known. . . . This righteousness is given through faith in Jesus Christ to all who believe. There is no difference between Jew and Gentile, for all have sinned and fall short of the glory of God, and all are justified freely by his grace through the redemption that came by Christ Jesus.
>
> Romans 3:21–24 NIV

We all have sinned and fallen short, yet through our faith in Jesus Christ we are freely justified by God's grace. Christ's righteousness for our sinfulness was the greatest exchange ever made—an exchange made at the cross and definitely all in our favor! God the Father made Jesus, who knew no sin, "to be sin for us, that we might become the righteousness of God in Him" (2 Corinthians 5:21). Now when the Father looks at us, He sees not our unworthy nature but the faultless righteousness of His Son.

We are not expected to be able to work our way up, gaining enough righteousness to finally achieve nirvana or some other exalted spiritual state. Neither do we anticipate untold years of suffering in purgatory after we die to become holy enough to enter heaven. We are all offered the great exchange—our sin for Jesus' righteousness. As soon as we who have accepted Christ's righteousness die, we go straight to heaven, into the presence of God.

As Paul pointed out in Romans 1:16–17, "The gospel, I say, can save men, for in it a way is revealed in which sinful men may be accepted before God and may stand in his presence approved and forgiven" (from George Barker Stevens's *The Epistles of Paul in Modern English*, Verploegh Editions, 1980). I like that—we are approved and forgiven. My favorite translation of this passage, the C. S. Lovett version, says, "The Gospel is power which emanates from God and saves all who believe in it . . . it reveals God's way of making men as righteous as Himself" (*Lovett's Lights on Romans*, Personal Christianity, 1992). God gave us His own righteousness.

Knowing we are righteous is a mighty weapon of our warfare. Righteousness empowers our prayers and enables us to approach God's throne boldly, with confidence that He will hear us. "The prayer of a righteous person is powerful and effective," says James 5:16 (NIV).

Righteousness also protects us. The devil cannot find any way to condemn us when Jesus' righteousness stands between us and judgment. Paul was right when he said, "We use the weapons of righteousness, in the right hand for attack and the left hand for defense" (2 Corinthians 6:7 NLT).

Be Baptized in Water and the Holy Spirit

For any believer, baptism is a powerful way to disarm the devil. Jesus was baptized in water by John the Baptist in the Jordan River, and there the Spirit of God also descended on Him like a dove (see Matthew 3:13–16). Jesus told His disciples believers should be baptized: "Go therefore and make disciples of all the nations, baptizing them in the name of the Father and of the Son and of the Holy Spirit" (Matthew 28:19). Not long after, Peter urged new believers, "Repent, and let every one of you be baptized in the name of Jesus Christ for the remission of sins; and you shall receive the gift of the Holy Spirit" (Acts 2:38). You arm yourself well against the devil when you follow these biblical mandates.

The waters of baptism are by faith the place you leave behind old bondages, habits, fears and addictions. When pressed against the edge of the Red Sea, Moses told the Israelites, "The Egyptians whom you see today, you shall see again no more forever" (Exodus 14:13). That day the Egyptian army perished before their eyes in a watery grave. Likewise, you by faith leave your bondages, habits, fears and addictions in the watery grave of baptism. Forevermore, you will no longer be their slave!

Baptism breaks off oppression and the sins that beset you before you became saved. You leave all the trash from your life before Christ under the water, and you break the surface to "walk in newness of life" (Romans 6:4). Paul described it this way: "For you were buried with Christ when you were baptized. And with him you were raised to new life because you trusted the mighty power of God, who raised Christ from the dead" (Colossians 2:12 NLT).

At baptism you shed your old nature to become someone new from the inside out. "Therefore, if anyone is in Christ, he is a new creation; old things have passed away; behold, all things have become new" (2 Corinthians 5:17). Your old nature is dead and buried under the waters of baptism, and try though he might, the devil soon finds out he cannot take a dead person to court. He tries to accuse you based on your past sins and failures, only to find that the person you once were has died and been buried. It is no longer *you* who live; rather Christ lives in you (see Galatians 2:20).

The new person you are in Christ also has the righteousness of Christ, so the accuser is left without a leg to stand on. In Romans 6 Paul asked a couple of questions the devil still cannot answer: "How shall we who died to sin live any longer in it? Or do you not know that as many of us as were baptized into Christ Jesus were baptized into His death?" (verses 2–3). Just as Adam took each of us down with him in the fall, Jesus took us with Him to the cross:

> Our old man was crucified with Him, that the body of sin might be done away with, that we should no longer be slaves of sin. For he who has died has been freed from sin. Now if we died with Christ, we believe that we shall also live with Him. . . . Reckon yourselves to be dead indeed to sin, but alive to God in Christ Jesus our Lord.
>
> Romans 6:6–8, 11

Satan can no longer bring any charges against you, for "there is therefore now no condemnation to those who are in Christ Jesus, who do not walk according to the flesh, but according to the Spirit" (Romans 8:1). If you have not yet been baptized in water as a believer, I encourage you to be baptized immediately.

If you have been baptized, but perhaps it was long ago, you may be thinking, *I didn't know all that could happen at baptism—now it's over and it's too late for me.* I urge you to think again. Revisit that moment of baptism and claim all its benefits now by faith. They are retroactive! Baptism is like marriage in that regard. The longer you live in it, the more you learn about it, and the more you know, the more you grow.

Nothing fills you with power from on high like God's Spirit dwelling within you. It is even dangerous to go against the devil without the Holy Spirit. Remember the last time Jesus appeared to His disciples after the resurrection? He gave them strict instructions not to make any move outside Jerusalem until they received the Holy Spirit: "And now I will send the Holy Spirit, just as my Father promised. But stay here in the city until the Holy Spirit comes and fills you with power from heaven" (Luke 24:49 NLT).

In a word, the Holy Spirit is indispensable. Jesus knew His disciples needed the Spirit's power to accomplish their task. Look how Jesus described the Spirit's purposes:

But the Comforter (Counselor, Helper, Intercessor, Advocate, Strengthener, Standby), the Holy Spirit, Whom the Father will send in My name [in My place, to represent Me and act on My behalf], He will teach you all things. And He will cause you to recall (will remind you of, bring to your remembrance) every-thing I have told you.

John 14:26 AMP

You need to be filled with the Holy Spirit. The Holy Spirit within you overpowers the devil, for "greater is he that is in you, than he that is in the world" (1 John 4:4 KJV).

Align Your Words with God's Word

If you want to walk in the victory Jesus purchased for you, align your words with God's Word and *speak out your faith*. Psalm 107:2 says, "Let the redeemed of the LORD *say so*, whom He has redeemed from the hand of the enemy" (italics added). Your faith is released through your words.

Can words really disarm the devil? Absolutely! Your spoken word is vital. Revelation 12:11 states, "They [believers] over-came him [Satan] by the blood of the Lamb and by the word of their testimony." When Jesus returns, He will defeat His enemies with a two-edged sword coming out of His mouth (see Revelation 1:16).

"Two-edged" in the Greek can actually be translated "two-tongued," and you have that same "two-tongued" sword at your disposal. First God says something—that is the first tongue. Then you speak in agreement with God's Word—that is the second tongue. When you verbally align your words with God's Word, that two-edged sword has the same power it had coming out of Jesus' mouth. God's Word in your mouth is the sword of the Spirit. It defeats your enemies, too.

Teaching His disciples about faith, Jesus said,

> Have faith in God. *For assuredly*, I say to you, *whoever says* to this mountain, "Be removed and be cast into the sea," and does not doubt in his heart, but believes that those things he says will be done, *he will have whatever he says.*

Mark 11:22–23, italics added

Whoever says something in faith according to the Word of God will "assuredly" have whatever he or she says. In other translations, Jesus says "verily, verily" or "truly" or "for sure." Note Jesus did not say "maybe, maybe" or "sometimes, sometimes" or "perhaps" this will work. He said it will assuredly work.

Jesus said this will work for *whoever*, and that means you or me or any believer. This will work for the simplest person you know. Do not listen to the lies, "This won't work for you. You're not smart enough; you're not holy enough; you're not rich enough; you're the wrong gender; you're the wrong race." Those are Satan's lies. The truth? It will work—if you use it.

Alas, having a sword at your disposal does not guarantee victory. You must *wield* it to win battles. The powerful combination of your faith plus your words will not work if you keep your mouth shut. You need to speak to the mountains in your life, knowing that Jesus said you will have what you *say*.

Instead of using this truth to their advantage, many Christians affect their lives negatively by what they say. They exchange the sword of the Spirit, the Word of God, for a sword of doubt and negativity, and they turn that weapon on themselves. They say, "I'll probably catch the flu," or "This weakness runs in my family," or "I don't have enough money for the rent," or "My marriage will never change." On and on they go, and then they blame God because they cannot experience victory.

The horrible thing for those who keep saying what they have is that they keep getting what they've got. Think carefully about that. Instead of speaking in faith, they speak in doubt and reap what their words have sown. God said, "I create the fruit of the lips" (Isaiah 57:19). That fruit can be bad or good—depending on you and your mouth.

If you want health, strength, blessings and victory in your life, let the words of your mouth agree with God's Word: "By his stripes I am healed" (Isaiah 53:5). "I can do all things through Christ who strengthens me" (Philippians 4:13). "God has blessed me with every spiritual blessing" (Ephesians 1:3). "When I resist the devil in Jesus' name, he *will* flee" (James 4:7). A Bible full of God's promises waits for you. Every one of them is "yes" and "amen" for you (see 2 Corinthians 1:20). When you align your words with God's Word, you will reap the fruit of your lips, effectively stop the devil and walk in victory.

Be His Ambassador

When you and I recognize that we represent Jesus the Deliverer as ambassadors of the Kingdom of God, we announce Jesus' victory over the devil everywhere we go, to everyone we meet. Paul explained our mission as ambassadors this way:

> God has given us the privilege of urging everyone to come into his favor and be reconciled to him. For God was in Christ, restoring the world to himself, no longer counting men's sins against them but blotting them out. This is the wonderful message he has given us to tell others. We are Christ's ambassadors. God is using us to speak to you: we beg you, as though Christ himself were here pleading with you, receive the love he offers you—be reconciled to God.
>
> 2 Corinthians 5:18–20 TLB

As ambassadors, we are authorized to represent the Kingdom of God to the world. Although the world is Satan's domain,

1 John 4:4 assures us, "Greater is he that is in you, than he that is in the world" (KJV). Our testimony as ambassadors is one of the weapons with which we overcome the accuser (see Revelation 12:11).

"He has delivered us from the power of darkness," Paul tells us, "and conveyed us into the kingdom of the Son of His love" (Colossians 1:13). Although we live in this world, we have been translated out of the domain of darkness and into its opposite, the Kingdom of Light (which is the Kingdom of the Son of His love). Everywhere Light goes, darkness flees. The more we spread the wonderful news that God no longer counts men's sins against them but has made a way for them to be reconciled to Him, the more the Light in us dispels the darkness.

We live by the law of the Kingdom of God—to love one another. The devil hates it when we escape his domain, and he hates it twice as much when we love others and help them to also walk in Jesus' victory. The more people who walk in the Light, the more earthly ambassadors there are who demonstrate Satan's defeat.

Keep Your Passion Hot

Satan's kingdom is motivated by lust, greed and pride—things designed to pull us away from God. As 1 John 2:16 says, "For all that is in the world—the lust of the flesh, the lust of the eyes, and the pride of life—is not of the Father but is of the world." We guard our hearts against those things by staying focused on seeking first the Kingdom of God. Look at *The Message* version of that passage:

> Don't love the world's ways. Don't love the world's goods. Love of the world squeezes out love for the Father. Practically everything that goes on in the world—wanting your own way, wanting

everything for yourself, wanting to appear important—has nothing to do with the Father. It just isolates you from him. The world and all its wanting, wanting, wanting is on the way out—but whoever does what God wants is set for eternity.

1 John 2:15–17

Our passion for the things of God disarms the devil's ability to distract us with wanting the wrong things, things that isolate us from God.

We all have natural desires for some of the things of this world—nourishment for our bodies, a place to live and rest, rejuvenating sleep, beauty around us, companionship and even a sense of self-worth. None of these things are evil in themselves. It is the frenzied striving after these things that causes trouble. Many people's lives revolve around the very things God told us *not* to strive after—understandably so, given that the world's passion for food, drink, fashion and fulfillment is promoted conspicuously on nearly every Internet site, billboard and TV commercial. But God promised to give us everything we need if we will seek instead after the things of His Kingdom:

> Therefore do not worry, saying, "What shall we eat?" or "What shall we drink?" or "What shall we wear?" For after all these things the Gentiles seek. For your heavenly Father knows that you need all these things. But seek first the kingdom of God and His righteousness, and all these things shall be added to you.

Matthew 6:31–33

Serving God and letting Him meet our needs keeps lust, greed and pride from knocking us off balance. Passion for God is protection from the devil. If we take our minds off our task and start chasing after the world, though, we put ourselves in danger. When our passion heats up toward the world's riches, it cools down toward God. The result is a lukewarm spirit that puts us in danger not only from the devil, but from God Himself. God warns the lukewarm,

> I know your works, that you are neither cold nor hot. . . . Because you are lukewarm, and neither cold nor hot, I will vomit you out of My mouth. . . . You say, "I am rich, have become wealthy, and have need of nothing"—and do not know that you are wretched, miserable, poor, blind, and naked.
>
> Revelation 3:15–17

Not that there is anything wrong with material wealth. Money is neutral—neither good nor bad. It is simply a tool, and it also reveals what is already in someone's heart. Suppose a drug dealer drops a bag of money downtown while running from the police. I find it and turn it in, but nobody claims it, so the police give it back to me. That money will not corrupt me when I take it home. I will not experience a sudden irresistible desire to hide behind my garage and smoke marijuana. That money revealed the evil in the drug dealer's heart when *he* used it to do harmful, illegal things. But in *my* hands it will reveal what is in my heart—a desire to do good with it and bless the Kingdom of God.

Love of money is what the Bible calls a root of all kinds of evil (see 1 Timothy 6:10). A passion for worldly wealth gets people into trouble, for it supplants passion for God. "No one can serve two masters. Either you will hate the one and love the other, or you will be devoted to the one and despise the other. You cannot serve both God and money" (Matthew 6:24 NIV).

This is an either/or situation. We either serve God and keep the things of this world in proper perspective, or we serve our desire for the things of this world and lose our proper perspective on the Kingdom of God. We need to give the devil no foothold by keeping our passion hot for God. Our daily, constant focus on God invites His desires in us and disarms the devil's ability to distract us with destructive desires birthed by lust, greed and pride. "Delight yourself also in the LORD," Psalm 37:4 tells us, "and He shall give you the desires of your heart."

The Whole Armor of God

God provided us with far more than one or two weapons with which we can experience Jesus' victory over the devil. He equipped us with a full suit of armor for spiritual battle. "Therefore take up the whole armor of God, that you may be able to withstand in the evil day, and having done all, to stand" (Ephesians 6:13). In this chapter we have followed that directive. We have put on the whole armor Ephesians 6 describes:

> Stand firm then, with the belt of truth buckled around your waist, with the breastplate of righteousness in place, and with your feet fitted with the readiness that comes from the gospel of peace. In addition to all this, take up the shield of faith, with which you can extinguish all the flaming arrows of the evil one. Take the helmet of salvation and the sword of the Spirit, which is the word of God.
>
> Verses 14–17 NIV

The belt of knowing the truth supports and strengthens us. God's truths have helped us size up our enemy and understand how to resist him.

The breastplate of Christ's righteousness covers us so we are blessed and not cursed. We left our sin natures under the waters of baptism, and now, baptized by the Holy Spirit, we are filled with power from on high.

Our feet are ready to carry the good news of Jesus' victory over the devil to others.

Our shield of faith is impenetrable because we believe not only in Jesus but also in the power of Jesus' name. Nothing in heaven, on earth or under the earth can stand against the authority we have been given in that name.

The helmet of salvation marks our allegiance—we are transferred from the kingdom of darkness into the Kingdom of Light.

We wield the two-edged sword of the Spirit by aligning our faith-filled words with God's Word.

In addition to all those mighty spiritual weapons, as we put first God's Kingdom and keep our passion hot for the things of God, He provides us with everything else we need. He has provided all the tools and weapons we need to walk in the victory Jesus the Deliverer purchased for us.

Jesus said, "Fear not, little flock; for it is your Father's good pleasure to give you the kingdom" (Luke 12:32 KJV). But He also said, "The kingdom of heaven suffers violence, and the violent take it by force" (Matthew 11:12). Which verse is true? Both! That explains why putting on the whole armor of God is so important. While God wants to give us the Kingdom, Satan will try to stand in the way. He will try to steal from, kill and destroy our families, our health, our finances or any area he thinks he can infiltrate. Although we are God's flock, we also need to be soldiers in God's army. We need to exert the energy necessary to resist the devil, who tries to keep us from receiving and walking in all God has for us.

"Be prepared. You're up against far more than you can handle on your own. Take all the help you can get, every weapon God has issued, so that when it's all over but the shouting you'll still be on your feet," says *The Message* translation of Ephesians 6:13. It is up to us to take all the help God has supplied—to take up the weapons we have studied in this chapter and use them to show the devil he has been disarmed.

Jesus the Deliverer Leads Us in Triumph

God has well equipped us to "still be on our feet" at the end of our spiritual campaign. We know His plan is for us to demonstrate Satan's defeat, and Jesus our Deliverer "always leads us in triumph in Christ" (2 Corinthians 2:14).

Do you recall the Roman Triumph I described earlier, in which the triumphator paraded gloriously through the streets of Rome? Clad in royal robes, he rode in a gilded chariot, while around him carts overflowed with the spoils of war. In front were his vanquished enemies, bound in chains and forced to walk in humiliating defeat. There is one detail I have yet to mention about the grand spectacle. The returning commander's troops, the battle-weary but victorious champions of his campaign, shared in his Triumph. Some followed his chariot and carried placards describing him or maps showing the territories he vanquished. Some led the carts of rich spoil. Still others preceded him and kept the chain-bound prisoners in line. All around him, those soldiers who were still standing on their feet when it was all over also enjoyed the people's accolades as they paraded home in victory with their commander.

That is a magnificent picture of how Christ always leads us in triumph. "In the Messiah, in Christ, God leads us from place to place in one perpetual victory parade. Through us, he brings knowledge of Christ. Everywhere we go, people breathe in the exquisite fragrance," says 2 Corinthians 2:14 (MESSAGE).

That fragrance is the fragrance of victory, the fragrance of Christ in us bringing salvation and freedom and healing and blessing everywhere we go, as we disarm the devil and demonstrate Satan's defeat.

9

Enlisting in God's Army

How to Receive Salvation

We have covered a lot of ground—in fact, we have *taken* a lot of ground for God's Kingdom—as we have sized up our enemy, studied his weaknesses and tactics and learned how to disarm him. To help you effectively demonstrate Satan's defeat from now on, I have one very important matter still to cover. I want to make certain you have enlisted in the army of God so that you can reap the benefits of giving your allegiance to the Lord of lords and transferring your citizenship from the kingdom of darkness to the Kingdom of heaven.

Come Into the Light

The whole world is under the influence of the evil one. Satan is the god (small g!) of this world, and he is a terrible taskmaster. He cares nothing for the well-being of those under his domain—after all, he wants them dead. "The wages of sin is death," says Romans 6:23. Or, as *The Message* translation puts it, you can "work hard for sin your whole life and your pension is death."

If you have never made Jesus the Lord of your life, it is time to transfer your allegiance to a new Lord and take up your citizenship in a new Kingdom. This is your day to experience the power of Jesus the Deliverer in your life!

If at some point you made Jesus Lord but have since gone AWOL and drifted back into the world, it is time for you to reenlist in God's army. "Come, and let us return to the LORD," urges Hosea 6:1. No matter where you have been or what you have done, you simply need to repent and return, and He will welcome you back with open arms.

Finally, if you *think* you are serving God and *hope* you will get into heaven when you die, it is time for you to make certain. You can never live a good enough life, pray enough or fast enough to earn your place in God's Kingdom. Your new life there is a free gift Jesus already purchased at the cross. You need only receive it so that, according to God's Word, you "*know* that you have eternal life" (1 John 5:13, italics added).

Whether you are a newcomer to Christ, an AWOL believer or someone unsure of where you stand with God, why should you serve a life sentence of hard labor in the kingdom of darkness when you can come into the Kingdom of Light? "The free gift of God is eternal life through Christ Jesus our Lord" (Romans 6:23 NLT). Just for the asking, you can be transferred into God's Kingdom and belong to Him. You can be saved, healed, set free and blessed from this moment on.

God promised, "Whoever calls on the name of the LORD shall be saved" (Romans 10:13). *Whoever* includes *you*. Pray the following prayer out loud from your heart—for "if you confess with your mouth that Jesus is Lord and believe in your heart that God raised him from the dead, you will be saved" (Romans 10:9 NLT).

> O God, I come to You in Jesus' name. I believe that Jesus died on the cross, shed His precious blood and paid for my sins. I receive Your forgiveness for all my sins. I believe that Jesus rose again, so right now I receive Him as Lord of my life. I am not going to live to please myself any longer. I am going to live for Jesus every day. Devil, you just lost me; Jesus, I am Yours! Heavenly Father, I thank You that You have heard my prayer. Thank You that, according to Your Word, my sins are forgiven, my past is gone, I am Your child and I am on my way to heaven! In Jesus' name, Amen.

You just made the most important decision of your life, and you will never be the same. You are now a citizen of God's Kingdom and an heir to all the precious promises in His Word. You have full authority in Jesus' name, so this is your day to start demonstrating Satan's defeat!

You can go to sleep tonight knowing for certain that your sins are forgiven, you are a child of God and you are on your way to heaven. If you have further questions or need personal assistance to help you on your way, our contact information is listed on the author biography page at the back of this book. Welcome to the family of God! Welcome to the Triumph of Jesus Christ!

Reference Guide

The following summary is a guide to the important lists we have worked through, including the spiritual laws the devil cannot break, things he cannot do to believers, tactics for disarming him and some others. I have included it so that the spiritual principles we have learned will be easily accessible any time you need to refresh your memory at a moment's notice or help others in need. The guide includes chapter numbers and section titles so you can quickly refer back to a portion of text when necessary. I trust having these lists at your fingertips will help you not only stand against the enemy but also advance and take ground for God's Kingdom.

Remember, the enemy has fallen and the advantage is on your side. You are delivered and protected, and victory is yours in Jesus' name. May the King of kings always lead you in triumph!

Spiritual Laws the Devil Cannot Break (Chapter 3)

Some things never change: God has ordained certain spiritual laws that the devil simply cannot bypass.

1. The Devil Cannot Be Like God

There is only one Savior, one Lord, Jesus Christ. The devil is a God wannabe who longs for the worship and allegiance that belong only to God, but he is nothing like God and never will be.

2. The Devil Cannot Understand the Ways and Word of God

The Bible and the ways of God must be understood spiritually by the revelation of God's Holy Spirit. That counts the devil out. His defeat is clearly recorded in the prophecies of Scripture, although he does not yet comprehend it.

3. The Devil Cannot Resist the Name of Jesus

There is nothing that does not bow to the name of Jesus, and that includes the devil. Jesus' name is above every other name.

4. The Devil Cannot Stop the Power of the Gospel

The Gospel *is* the power of God. Salvation goes beyond forgiveness to include healing, deliverance, peace, restoration and everything else we need. The devil cannot stop any of the blessings inherent in the Gospel from coming your way.

5. The Devil Cannot Escape Revelation 20:10

The devil is headed for the lake of fire mentioned in Revelation 20:10. When he tries to show you your sorry past, show him his sorry future instead. The devil cannot escape Revelation 20:10, but as a believer you already have!

6. The Devil Cannot Get Saved

Salvation is for the "seed of Abraham," those in a flesh-and-blood body. You need to choose salvation before you die. Spirits without physical bodies—such as the devil—cannot get saved.

7. *The Devil Cannot Predict the Future*

The devil is a finite, created being. He is not omniscient, or all-knowing, like God. He cannot predict his own future accurately, much less predict yours!

8. *The Devil Cannot Operate in an Atmosphere of Praise*

Praise is demon repellant; it stops the devil and his forces in their tracks. It brings confusion to the demonic realm and releases angelic ministry.

9. *The Devil Cannot Withstand the United Assault of the Church*

Everything God does on earth He does through the Church, and Jesus said the gates of hell would not prevail against it (see Matthew 16:18).

Things the Devil Cannot Do to Believers (Chapter 4)

Believers are protected by law—God's law. The devil is severely limited in what he can do to God's children when they stay safely within their good Shepherd's care.

10. *The Devil Cannot Touch Your Spirit*

The Holy Spirit seals you at salvation, and the devil cannot go through the blood of the Lamb to get to you. Your spirit belongs to God alone.

11. *The Devil Cannot Violate Your Free Will*

There is no such excuse as "the devil made me do it." He cannot make you do anything. God gave each person a free will—Satan cannot violate it, and God will not violate it. Every day, every minute, you have the right to choose whom you will serve.

12. The Devil Cannot Possess What You Do Not Yield

The devil must seek those whom he devours. He cannot gain access into your life unless you yield it. When you obey God, live by His Word and resist the devil, he *must* flee.

13. The Devil Cannot Stay Where He Is Not Welcome

Like a stray dog, the devil cannot settle in your house unless you open the door to him. Sin lets the devil in, but resistance in Jesus' name drives him away.

14. The Devil Cannot Trespass Unless You Let Him

The devil has no legal right to set foot on your spiritual property. He may try to trespass from time to time, but he cannot dump trash from the kingdom of darkness on you anymore. You, however, must possess and defend your Promised Land in the Kingdom. Repel Satan's attacks and put up "No Trespassing" signs.

15. The Devil Cannot Hide from the Word of God in You

When you have the Word of God inside you, you are not easily misled by the devil's schemes, even if he disguises himself as an angel of light. Not everything that happens is God's will, and you need to know the Word so you can properly discern what comes from God and what does not.

16. The Devil Cannot Get You to Blame God When You Know the Word

The devil cannot get you to blame God for the bad things in life if you know the Word. Satan would love to get people mad at God, but knowing the truth—*Good God, bad devil*—will keep you from falling into that trap. Jesus came that you might have life abundantly, whereas anything that steals from, kills or destroys you is of the devil (see John 10:10, the "great divide" verse).

Exposing the Enemy's Weaknesses (Chapter 5)

Knowing the enemy's weaknesses gives you insight into how to overcome him. The more familiar you are with the things the devil cannot do to you personally, the less familiar you will be with his interference in your life.

17. *The Devil Cannot Separate You from the Love of God*

Nothing can separate you from God's love—you cannot even separate yourself from it! Whether you are the greatest of saints or the worst of sinners, God's love for you remains the same, and the devil cannot do anything about it.

18. *The Devil Cannot Bless You*

Everyone and everything the devil touches tends toward destruction, bondage and decay. He has no blessings to offer, and why would you want any of his curses?

19. *The Devil Cannot Keep You Depressed*

Depression is a widely used tool of the enemy, but not an invincible one. God offers us the garment of praise for the spirit of heaviness (see Isaiah 61:3). Thanksgiving magnifies our perception of God and minimizes our problems, so turn to praise and thanksgiving when attacks of depression come your way.

20. *The Devil Cannot Condemn You Unless You Let Him*

The devil, the "accuser of the brethren," is forever throwing condemnation in the face of believers. He would like you to lay down your righteousness in Christ and give way to despair and defeat; but Jesus justified you, so there is now no condemnation for you (see Romans 8:1).

21. *The Devil Cannot Take You to Hell If You Do Not Want to Go*

If you accept Christ, you become a citizen of God's Kingdom. No matter how much the devil may want to take you to hell, he *cannot*! When you choose Jesus as Lord, the devil loses all claim on you, and you are headed for heaven, not hell.

The Question of Curses (Chapter 6)

The devil and his hordes *cannot* attach a curse to God's people without cause. There is not a devil, demon or satanist in existence who can put a curse on God's children whom He has blessed. It will not "stick." You can, however, bring a curse upon yourself. Following are some ways you can give a curse a cause.

Idol Worship Invites a Curse

Any involvement in false religions opens a door to the occult, because behind all false gods are demon spirits. Any dabbling in ideologies that lift up or worship something other than the one true God will lead you down a destructive road.

Sexual Immorality Invites a Curse

Illicit or perverse sexual practices usher in a curse, because when two people join in the physical, a bridge forms between them in the spiritual. Bondages can and do cross over.

Anti-Semitism Invites a Curse

God promised to bless those who bless Israel and curse those who curse it (see Genesis 12:3). Anti-Semitism is a demonic spirit. Jesus Himself was Jewish, so if you have a problem with the Jews, you have a problem with the Savior.

Robbing God Invites a Curse

Robbing God in tithes and offerings brings a curse (see Malachi 3:9). Better to live on 90 percent of your income with God's blessing than on 100 percent with a curse!

Negative Words Invite a Curse

Your spoken word sets creative forces in motion. God creates the fruit of your lips, whether good or rotten (see Isaiah 57:19). Negative words give Satan license to try to bring those destructive things you talk about into your life, whereas faith-filled words move the heart of God.

Uncovering the Enemy's Tactics (Chapter 7)

What does it look like when people give a curse a cause or open the door to the devil? Demonic spirits can and do infiltrate and destroy the lives of people who live outside the protection we enjoy as believers. Here we look at a dozen signs of demonic activity in people's lives, as demonstrated in the Gadarene demoniac whom Jesus delivered.

Sign 1: Withdrawal from Social Interaction

Severe and continual withdrawal from social interaction can indicate something sinister is afoot. If the devil can isolate people, he can devour them. The first banana that breaks off the bunch is the first one eaten.

Sign 2: A Tormented Mental State

It is not normal to suffer such pronounced mental distress that you would do anything, from self-mutilation to suicide, to be free of your thoughts, yet that is the state of many people today. A tormented mind is a sure sign of demon trouble.

Sign 3: Chronic Depression

The devil would like you to feel so worthless that you do not see the priceless value God sets on you, and you take your own life. Death is Satan's ultimate goal for every person, and chronic depression is an insidious tool he will use toward that end.

Sign 4: Irrational Fears and Phobias

Demons are fearful (as in, *they* are frightened), and they like to spread fear around, causing people who do not aggressively apply God's Word to succumb to irrational fears and phobias. God has not given us a spirit of fear, but of power and love and a sound mind (see 2 Timothy 1:7).

Sign 5: Chronic Restlessness

A constant urgency to be on the move can signal demonic activity. The Gadarene demoniac was always restless, never at peace. The saying "No God, no peace; know God, know peace" is absolutely true.

Sign 6: Unclean Desires and Lewd Behavior

Unclean desires and lewd or immodest behavior strongly indicate demonic activity. They pollute a life just as muddy water pollutes clean water, but in our society you will not automatically know this unless you are taught it from the Bible.

Sign 7: Addictive and Compulsive Behaviors

Any behavior that so captures someone that they cannot break away from it under their own power indicates demonic involvement. Obvious examples include alcohol and drug abuse, uncontrollable gambling and involvement in illicit sex or pornography, but there are numerous other examples.

Sign 8: Uncontrollable Rage

People who bottle up anger on the inside until they explode have given the devil a foothold. Whenever someone flies off the handle time after time in uncontrollable rage, it is a probable sign of demonic activity.

Sign 9: Violent Behavior

Extreme and unwarranted violence signal demonic forces at work. The violent Gadarene demoniac did not break off his chains under his own power.

Sign 10: A Fixation on Death and the Occult

Though God instilled in people a natural aversion to death, the Gadarene lived among the dead. A fixation on death signifies demonic activity, as does a fixation on the occult and occult symbols.

Sign 11: Suicidal Thoughts

Suicidal thoughts are a sure sign of the demonic. Demonic forces extinguish the desire to live. Anything that makes death appealing originates from the kingdom of darkness.

Sign 12: Absolute Helplessness

Sometimes people reach the point of absolute helplessness. They have done all they can think of to escape their bondages, but despite all their efforts, nothing changes. That signals demonic sabotage.

Twelve Signs, One Cure

The Lord hears and answers the call of every sincere heart. He does not despise anyone who has been wounded or taken prisoner of war by the enemy. Jesus came to destroy the devil's works and to provide us with weapons to disarm the devil.

Jesus the Deliverer (Chapter 8)

Jesus the Deliverer always leads us in triumph. Jesus triumphed over Satan once and for all at the cross, and then He exclaimed, "It is finished!" (John 19:30). Through His death, burial, resurrection and ascension He provided us with numerous powerful spiritual weapons that disarm the devil. Let's put on the full armor of God and use the weapons He provided!

Take Authority in the Name of Jesus

The first and foremost weapon you can wield to demonstrate Satan's defeat is your authority in Jesus' name. When you belong to Jesus, the power in His name belongs to you. Everything that has a name (whether cancer, depression, poverty or anything else) has to bow to the name of Jesus, so you need to speak out His mighty name.

Know the Truth

The Bible contains 31,101 truth-revealing verses. A knowledge of the truths in God's Word is a powerful weapon with which you can stand against the enemy and gain your spiritual freedom. The devil cannot stand against the Word of God.

Identify the Enemy

"Know your enemy" is an important military principle. If you identify your enemy, familiarize yourself with his tactics of war and wield the weapons Jesus has provided to disarm him, you will experience victory.

Resist, Resist, Resist

How do you resist the devil? You resist with your words, your actions and your choices. Using your authority in Jesus' name is your first line of resistance against the devil.

Understand You Were Transferred at Salvation

When you got saved, your transfer went through. God rescued you from the devil's kingdom and transferred you into His own Kingdom. The claims the kingdom of darkness had on you ended as soon as your citizenship changed to the Kingdom of Light.

Know You Are Blessed, Not Cursed

Anything under the curse of the Law does not belong in your life (see Deuteronomy 28; Galatians 3:13). The benefits, or blessings, of God now belong to you—all His many promises are "yes and amen" for you.

Put On Righteousness

Christ's righteousness for your sinfulness was the greatest exchange made at the cross. His righteousness in you is a mighty weapon of your warfare that enables you to approach God's throne boldly, with confidence that He will hear you.

Be Baptized in Water and the Holy Spirit

Baptism with water and the Spirit is a powerful way to disarm the devil. Baptism in water breaks off oppression and sin, and nothing fills you with power from on high like God's Spirit dwelling within you. The Holy Spirit is indispensable.

Align Your Words with God's Word

If you want victory over the devil, align your words with the two-edged sword of God's Word and speak out your faith. Your faith plus your words is a powerful combination vital in overcoming the devil. Remember, God creates the fruit of your lips (see Isaiah 57:19).

Be His Ambassador

You and I become mighty weapons to disarm the devil in other people's lives when we serve as ambassadors for the Kingdom. Pleading with people to be reconciled to God, you plunder hell and populate heaven.

Keep Your Passion Hot

Passion for God is protection from the devil. When you seek first God's Kingdom, your Father provides you with everything else you need.

The Whole Armor of God

God equipped us with a whole suit of armor for spiritual battle. We need to take all the help we can get, every weapon

God has issued for spiritual battle, so when it is all over but the shouting, we are still standing (see Ephesians 6:10–20).

Jesus the Deliverer Leads Us in Triumph

God has well equipped us to still be on our feet at the end of our spiritual campaign. "In the Messiah, in Christ, God leads us from place to place in one perpetual victory parade" (2 Corinthians 2:14 MESSAGE).

Jesus the Deliverer always leads us in triumph! Everywhere we go, Christ in us brings salvation and freedom and healing and blessing as we disarm the devil at every turn. May we go on from here to demonstrate Satan's defeat and share in the Triumph of Jesus the Deliverer every day of our lives.

Other Books by Duane Vander Klok

Get the Junk Out of Your Trunk (Chosen, 2005)
Your heart is like a trunk, a suitcase you carry every day. What fills your trunk? Nothing hinders spiritual growth as much as carrying a little unforgiveness around in your trunk. In this book, Pastor Duane shows you how to recognize unforgiveness and bitterness in your life. He shows you how Scripture can help you clean such junk out of your trunk and fill it with good things so that you can experience the peace and victory God has in store for you.

Unleashing the Force of Favor (Chosen, 2006)
God's favor is freely given to every believer, yet many live without seeing its full force at work in their lives. While favor is not a formula, you can take steps to grow in favor, as Jesus did. In this book, Pastor Duane offers practical, scriptural advice on the importance of raising your expectations about favor, believing God's favor is *for you* and letting your faith move your mouth so that you can grow in favor with God and with the people around you. God means for you to enjoy His mighty favor in every area of life!

Your New Life (Resurrection Life Church Publishing, 2005)
Developing your new life in Christ is the single most important thing this side of heaven. In this book, Pastor Duane talks to new believers about how to walk out their new life, how to grow spiritually and become strong and how to find a church body to serve in where they will be loved and supported in their faith. If you are a new believer, this book is key to getting off to a great start as you begin living for the Lord and walking in His blessings.

Pastor Duane Vander Klok and his wife, Jeanie, attended Christ For The Nations Institute, then served on the mission field in Mexico for seven years. In 1984 they returned to the United States to pastor Resurrection Life Church in Grandville, Michigan, where they have been ever since. Resurrection Life Church has a weekly attendance of approximately 8,000 people.

Resurrection Life Churches International, founded by Pastor Duane, is involved in church planting and has over 75 affiliate churches around the world.

Pastor Duane also hosts a weekly television program called *Walking by Faith*, which now reaches locally and globally through television and the Internet across the U.S. and in over 249 nations around the world. For more information, visit www.walkingbyfaith.tv.

Duane and Jeanie's family includes three sons and a daughter, their spouses and thirteen grandchildren.